DEAR

I PR[...]
WILL BE [...]
TO YOU!

Love
A[...]

1

SOLOMON'S RECIPE

FINDING TRUST IN AN UNTRUSTWORTHY WORLD

Reading Solomon's Recipe, I found myself engrossed to the point that I was a part of the story . . . Amazingly, through the magic of Allan's expression based on real life experiences Solomon's Recipe provided calming proof spoken by Moses when he stated "Fear ye not, stand still and see the salvation of the Lord (Exodus 14: 13). This book reminds me that . . . . the best thing to do is place the situation at the feet of our Lord and Savior. I highly recommend and endorse this book as a truthful real read for those who profess to do the work of the Lord.
Rev. Dr. Jerry Moore Sr., Moore Ministries

"Solomon's Recipe" sets forth a way of living shaped by Allan's reflections on his personal experiences in light of the Book of Proverbs. Surely Allan senses the range and depth of experiences, yours and mine, which are illuminated by moments and meanings he shares from his life. Some of Allan's experiences called to mind experiences of mine so vividly, I couldn't read them fast enough!
The Rev. Fred Thayer, Rector (Ret.)
St Bartholomew's Episcopal Church, Poway, CA

Solomon's Recipe is catchy title, but so much more than that. Through insights gained over a long lifetime, the author gently guides the reader through the ongoing challenges of learning—and relearning—trust in God. The "recipe," based on the biblical book of Proverbs, is creative and inspirational. Chapters contain true life stories and practical questions seen through the lens of Solomon's Recipe. This is a great book to read, and to share. It's a recipe everyone can follow.
The Rev. Dr Kathleen Long Bostrom
Author and Retired Minister (PCUSA)

Solomon's Recipe is an inspiring book that is filled with hope for men and women of all ages. The passages of scriptures used for Solomon's Recipe will challenge you and bless you beyond your wildest dreams if you follow the instructions. The true-life stories in the book are a constant reminder that with God all things are possible.
Rev. Rick Rojas Associate Pastor Shepherd's Pasture Assembly and Chaplain National City Police Department

SOLOMONS RECIPE

Dedication

I dedicate this book to my lovely wife, Carol

and to my wonderful son, Randy.

Table of Contents

With total trust in God, one is prepared for everything and surprised by nothing.

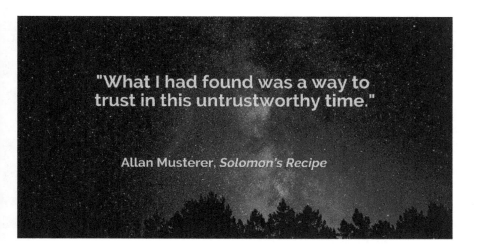

"What I had found was a way to trust in this untrustworthy time."

Allan Musterer, *Solomon's Recipe*

Introduction

My life has spanned eight decades. In that time, I have witnessed amazing progress and discoveries in medicine, artistry, psychology, technology, engineering, and science. Despite these advances that have made living in the world so much easier, life continues to present all of us with daunting challenges. We still struggle daily. We all face the tragic loss of loved ones, life-and-death crises, betrayals by those we trusted, lifelong hopes dashed, and catastrophic events that can change our lives profoundly—and in an instant. Many see life as difficult and turbulent. But it need not be so lonely, scary, or painful.

My experience has shown me that there are four main reasons why we struggle when we face life's greatest challenges. First, we are reluctant to trust; second, we insist on understanding; third, we ignore or dismiss the higher power as "luck"; and fourth, we refuse to look for guidance from the divine.

My life's work has taught me that there are a lot of people we meet who, though they presented themselves as trustworthy, turned out to be anything but. So, who do we trust? How do we find trust in an untrustworthy world?

We are set, with adamant insistence, in requiring that we understand everything we face before we find the courage to act. So, how do we find the courage of heart to act without first understanding? How do we navigate life positively while feeling blindfolded and without a compass of understanding?

We have this propensity to acknowledge "luck" when for some reason something "randomly" goes right for us. Then we are bound to the dilemma of contracting with this entity "luck" to shine on us more frequently or in a specifically critical moment. How do we accomplish that? How do we speak to "luck"? Where do we find it? Can we do something more that takes us beyond mere random chance?

We typically have thoughts like *I know what I am doing better than anyone. No one understands what I am going through. How will I know guidance when it comes to me and in what form will it be? How long will I have to wait? Will it come at all?* These thoughts and questions can leave us feeling paralyzed and stuck, or trapped in vehement resistance.

I have been blessed with a solution that can help anyone tackle these four obstacles to leading a life that can bring more harmony and joy. I call it Solomon's Recipe. The Recipe comes from the proverbs that are attributed to Solomon, King of Israel. This is where many of you might be feeling a rising sense of skepticism. You may have relegated anything Biblical to irrelevancy in your life. For those of you who are entertaining skepticism, I suggest you consider that something genuinely true, regardless of its source, will prove to be a benefit in navigating the storms and tides on your personal sea of life. Truth is true, regardless of where you find it.

Some may ask, "Why Solomon?" He was not perfect in how he lived his life. In fact, he violated some of the wisdom he himself penned for posterity. You may wonder, "Why should I put any credence in anything he has written?" To this I respond, "Because he was able to open himself to divine guidance." In fact, he asked for it. As a young teenager, Solomon had grown up watching his father, King David, enjoy a strong relationship with God and the benefits associated with it. In his youth, Solomon was placed into the great shoes of the King of Israel. Solomon, in a state of awe, naiveté, and humbleness, encountered God in a dream, who asked Solomon, "What shall I give you?" Don't let the gravity of that escape you. (1 Kings 3:5-9)

We often have this fantasy of some genie who comes out of a lamp and offers us three wishes that the genie supposedly has the power to grant. Unfortunately, we must face it: this is just fantasy. But the Creator, omnipotent, asked Solomon, "What shall I give you?"

Solomon responded, "Since I am so young and my task as king is so great, I need Your help! Give me a heart with the skill and sensitivity to listen when Your Holy Spirit comes to guide me."

God, impressed with such humbleness, gave Solomon what he asked for, plus the wisdom to act wisely.

Now, thousands of years later, the truths divinely revealed to Solomon are in the writings of his proverbs. These same truths are echoed in every ancient culture throughout the world. Every religion, every people across the globe, share these profound truths.

I have found that these verses in Proverbs offer a kind of recipe for acquiring access to the divine guidance that we all need to negotiate our unique life experience. My life is evidence for me that this Recipe works again and again with efficacy and consistency.

I hope you will walk with me and see how the truth in Solomon's Recipe can be the powerful force you have been seeking when facing both small and monumental life challenges. Be ready for miracles to open before you.

How I Found Solomon's Recipe

I was on the verge of a great adventure when I literally stumbled upon the words that would change my life. My dream was about to come true. I was leaving home to pursue my education that would launch me on a career in engineering. I had no idea what lay before me. I was young, naïve, and feeling prepared and confident. I was excited and eager to get on with it. Little did I know what was looming.

The Wednesday night before departing for college, my family and I attended church service just as we always did. I didn't think much of it, but it was the last service in our church that I would attend for almost three long months. In our church, each service began with a Bible passage. That passage became the foundation for the sermon message. On this evening, the passage was from Solomon's Proverbs, Chapter 3, verses 5 and 6.

I had always been impressed with Solomon, primarily because of his encounter with God as a teenager. I do not honestly recall how, on that evening, this passage from Proverbs impressed me or how the sermon based on it moved me. The future, however, revealed that it somehow got into me. It became a lifelong touchstone that has been a gold mine of wisdom and strength throughout my life to this day.

These words, in fact, became a life-changing recipe.

Solomon's Recipe Explained

Solomon's Recipe resides in Proverbs, chapter 3, verses 5 and 6. The King James Version of the Bible presents these verses as follows:

> *Trust in the LORD with all thine heart; and lean not unto thine own understanding.*

> *Proverbs 3:5*

> *In all thy ways acknowledge Him, and He shall direct thy paths.*

> *Proverbs 3:6*

For decades I have applied these words as a recipe for living, while facing both trivial and more serious life challenges. Like any recipe, it takes time and experience to get the final product just right. With Solomon's Recipe, each step builds upon the previous step. The success of the Recipe depends on developing an authentic trust in God. Without that, the Recipe fails. But experiencing a solid trust in God is often not an instantaneous experience. Often, people wonder if their trust in God is justified. Know that it is perfectly normal to have such doubts.

Also know this:

Each time you put the Recipe into practice, your trust will grow deeper. Your insistence on understanding will dissipate.

Acknowledging God becomes more comfortable and genuine, and most importantly, God's direction becomes more visible and real.

The more authentic and genuine the trust is, the more effective the Recipe will be in fulfilling its purpose, which is to gain guidance from the divine.

It's also important to understand that working with Solomon's Recipe takes practice, sometimes years of practice, to get it to work smoothly. As with any art, practice begins with "baby steps." You start off simply and then slowly become more advanced. Eventually, what was once new and difficult is performed with ease. This truth applies to practicing Solomon's Recipe.

As you begin applying the Recipe, you may find that you run up against what I call an "obstacle illusion." When you face an issue, it looks like the problem is outside of you. You become focused on the obstacle and it becomes hard to look beyond it. Now you find yourself stuck, mired in an attitude insisting that you must understand before you take another step.

The problem, however, is not the obstacle or the issue you are facing; it's you.

Your trust isn't deep enough, and you insist on understanding something that can't be understood at that particular moment.

This may preclude your ability to see God in control, and the divine guidance offered may be lost. What is at work here is that you are unwilling to turn over control of the challenging issue to an unseen God. That attitude screams, "Prove it!"

On the contrary, if you do allow yourself to step out of the way and to give the problem over to God to handle in God's time, you will experience a lightness of being. Know that it is perfectly normal and human to struggle with your trust in God, or to seek personal understanding time and time again. The goal is to gently move yourself toward a deeper trust of the Lord, instance by instance.

What you may find at first is that you need to practice the Recipe in facing smaller challenges before you practice it with bigger challenges. The reason is that it's easier to give up control when the consequences are less impactful. Your experience tackling small issues will provide you with the evidence that the Recipe works. The Recipe can then be applied to ever-increasing life struggles as you allow yourself to let go and let God do what He does best: help you through the most difficult challenges you will face.

~

A recipe has two components: ingredients and instructions. The ingredients define what elements make up the recipe, while the instructions define the sequence and timing of combining them. This is critical to achieving a successful end.

With this analogy in mind, I proceeded to analyze the words of this proverb, including the additions found in the Message Bible as follows:

> *Proverbs 3:5–6 (MSG): Trust GOD from the bottom of your heart; don't try to figure out everything on your own. Listen for GOD's voice in everything you do, everywhere you go; He's the one who will keep you on track. Don't assume that you know it all.*

I found the order of these four principles—trust God, don't try to figure it out on your own, listen for God's voice in everything you do, and don't assume you know it all—to be essential in integrating them into my thought processes. This is where trust came into play. Through experience, I learned that the Lord is trustworthy. He is faithful to me. Even when I didn't understand, the Lord always found a way to come through with something special and uniquely beneficial.

I also learned that applying this Recipe requires self-discipline. In this age of instant gratification, the "bake time" for this Recipe can test our resolve to slow down and wait for the perfect solution to be revealed. The heat in the oven can get challenging, but everything comes at the precise moment necessary for perfect resolution. Be patient.

~

There are amazing consequences when this recipe is followed. Here are some that I have experienced:

- Hidden talents and flaws are revealed
- Appreciation for life is increased in intensity
- True faithful friends are found
- Becoming a blessing to someone—a spouse, a child, a parent, a friend, a stranger—is put in motion
- Unexpected solutions to difficult decisions, situations, and problems become clear
- New people bring unexpected rewards
- Words of wisdom are found that significantly change thoughts and views

- Misunderstandings become clarified, bringing peaceful resolutions
- Painful experiences are soothed by revelations, resulting in the strength to endure
- Weaknesses of character are replaced with strength
- Profound truths are learned and can be shared to help others

It will be interesting to see what amazing consequences show up in your life when you exercise Solomon's Recipe. I hope you will pass them along.

~

Throughout the book, I will share with you how this Recipe has worked for me and for others that have touched my life.

I offer here a story that shows how quickly the Recipe can function; I call this experience Precise Positioning.

I felt trapped as I stood in the only available one square foot of space in the overcrowded emergency room. My wife, Carol, sat next to me on a folding chair at the foot of the hospital gurney that held her ninety-four-year old mother, Clara. I wondered what was going to happen next. *Why does God need me here?* I just knew something was up and God was going to use me, but how?

Earlier that afternoon, Carol and I had returned home from Sunday morning's church service where I served as a minister prior to my retirement. After a light lunch, Carol went to visit her mother. The week before, Clara had fallen at her assisted living facility. After a brief hospital stay, Clara was now at a rehabilitation facility, learning to walk again. She was going to need the assistance of a walker.

Friends from church had offered to give Clara a couple of walkers they no longer needed. I gratefully drove out to pick up the friends' walkers, loaded them into my car, and headed home.

I was about a third of the way there when my phone rang. It was Carol. She had just left the rehab center after visiting her mother when she got a call that Clara had fallen once again. An ambulance was coming to take her to the hospital emergency room. Although Clara did not sustain any noticeable injuries, hospital protocol required her to go to emergency. I told Carol I would meet them there.

I immediately prayed. First, I sincerely thanked God that Clara was not seriously hurt from her second fall. Then, feeling disappointed, I questioned God as to why it had to happen yet again! Hadn't He heard all my requests to keep her safe? No sooner did these words escape my lips when new words came to me.

"Okay Lord, I know there must be something important going on for this to happen again. I don't know what You have up Your sleeve, but I just want You to know I am going to keep my eyes open for whatever You have in store. I'm very curious how You will turn this fall of Clara's into good. Just give me the skills to listen for the whisper of Your Spirit."

Twenty minutes later, I arrived at the hospital just as the ambulance arrived. The EMTs wheeled Clara into the emergency room with Carol and me right behind. The emergency room was jam-packed; not a single room was free. Doctors and nurses rushed this way and that, trying to keep up. Clara was quickly examined and assessed as not critical. Her gurney was placed against the wall in the hallway. A folding chair for Carol was placed at the foot of Clara's gurney. Amidst the beehive of activity, I stood confined to a one-foot-square space next to Carol, against the wall. This was the only possible place for me to stand. Six inches either way and I would be blocking the busy corridor. I stood there for about fifteen minutes.

Suddenly a young lady came up to me, looked into my eyes, and asked, "Evangelist Musterer?"

I replied, "Yes."

She said, pointing, "If you look over there, just through the small crack in that curtain, you will see my mother. She was with you in church this morning. When she came home, she couldn't breathe. We called an ambulance to bring her here. She has been here for a while. She just woke up, and when she looked through the little crack in the curtain, she saw you. Will you please come and pray with her?"

"Of course," I said. "I will be honored."

I silently sent a prayer to God, thanking Him for sending me this blessing, and made my way to visit my friend. I smiled and shared with her what God had done in making it possible for me to be there for her. I prayed with her, thanking God for His awesome act of love and asking for His continued blessing for her health. I assured her that I would contact her minister and advise him of her situation while continuing to pray for her recovery.

I returned to my "station" and called the minister, who was out of town. I filled him in and he immediately made plans to visit our friend in the hospital. After a short stay, our friend was able to regain her strength, and she returned home.

Once Clara was examined by the doctors and all her tests proved normal, she was sent back to rehab. All day I thought of this experience and how God was able to get my attention to fulfill His purpose, offering assurance for a suffering soul that her God was there for her.

In my prayers for Clara's safety, I trusted God completely. But when that seemed to have failed, I did not understand. However, from previous experience I was able to reignite my trust and, without understanding, acknowledge God's hand in it. This allowed me to follow His guidance to that precise place for His purpose to be realized.

That's how the Recipe works for me and hopefully will for you too.

How to Make Solomon's Recipe Work for You

Practicing Solomon's Recipe is an art. As with every art, there are certain elements one must understand and appreciate in order to master that art. It's important to maintain a focus on the goal.

The goal of Solomon's Recipe is to open you up so that you can be more sensitive and responsive to divine guidance that will point you in the direction you are supposed to go. Once there, you will find yourself in the divine flow of life.

Also, as with any art, practice is required. Practice entails repeated exercise of the elements that make up the whole of the art. Practice requires patience, because mastering each element takes time. The more you practice, the more you will find that your successes will increase, and your failures will decrease.

As experiences mount, you will notice that there is a flow from one element to the next. The deeper you trust and the less understanding you insist upon, the more open and receptive you will become to the Lord's guidance.

This is the baking process.

~

You may ask," How does God convey or communicate His guidance?" While it may be a very personal experience, I can let you know that I have experienced God's guidance in the following ways:

- Feelings that are inconsistent with my norm. These feelings are not what I would normally expect. They stand out as extraordinary and signal something coming from a source external to me. That causes me to become alert and take notice.

- Someone says something to me that is unexpected and unusual. It sparks a curiosity and further deliberation to gain more understanding.
- A personal question is answered by a total stranger. Someone says something in a seemingly unconnected conversation, but it pointedly provides a long-sought-after answer.
- A book, movie, road sign, TV show, newspaper story, sermon, teacher, adage, or something common to me answers questions, gives advice, provides direction, or inspires a change in my thinking.
- I have an experience that seemingly happens out of the blue or feels like a perfectly timed "coincidence."
- I open the Bible to a random page and my eyes are drawn to a specific passage that provides clarity for a situation, a solution to a dilemma, an answer to a question, etc.
- An unexpected event occurs that changes everything—for example, when I have encountered surprising situations in my career, or with weather, or life events like births and deaths—giving new and different direction that leads to surprising benefits.
- Spontaneous thoughts inspire the new thought, *How does this fit?*
- Seeing something that isn't there—an apparition?
- I have dreams that can be a revelation in preparation for a new direction.
- In a sleepless night, a train of thoughts begins to flow through my semi-consciousness, revealing new understanding.

- Triggers arrive without warning. Smells, sights, or sounds inspire profound thoughts that can change my course, thoughts, or feelings.

The next question you might ask is," Why would God communicate with me?" What I have found is this:

- I asked for guidance.
- There is a need for me to change course and I am open to it.
- My plan is not the best plan for me.
- I am struggling and need help.
- Like Solomon, I asked for the skill to listen.

~

I am convinced that God will communicate with you, as He has with me, when you are ready. I challenge you to take the leap to trust God completely. Then, with anticipation and patience, watch for the guidance that will arrive.

One might think, *How can I trust an unseen God?* Consider that with all our reluctance to trust, we spontaneously and without thinking trust total strangers many times a day. When you stop your car at a traffic light, you implicitly trust that the stranger driving behind you is also going to stop. You trust that your doctor is in fact a licensed and properly educated medical professional. And the list goes on.

I have found that to really trust God, you must also conquer fear. I once delivered a sermon on fear, and in my research, I found that the phrase "fear not" is mentioned 365 times in the Bible. That is once a day for a year. I remember thinking, *How am I going to remember to eliminate fear every day?*

On my way home after the service, I came up with a solution. On a piece of white adhesive tape used for bandages, I wrote in bold black letters "FEAR NOT" and posted it on the face of my alarm clock. This ensured that the first words I saw each day could not be forgotten.

I wrote this book in the hope that as you, my dear reader, journey through these pages, you will see how my experiences have revealed the blessing of following Solomon's Recipe. My prayer is that the stories will trigger your own moments of self-discovery and prompt a new trust in God. As you embrace the Recipe with each challenge you face, peace, gratitude, and happiness in ever-increasing depth can follow.

Stress comes from trying to do it all on your own. Peace comes from putting it all in God's hands.

CHAPTER 1

FACING BIG DECISIONS

Life presents us with moments when we must make big, life-changing decisions. These moments of decision often come when we least expect them and at a time when we are not prepared. But the decisions must be made, and time is usually not on our side. What do we do? We worry, we get emotionally distraught, and in the heat of the moment we make that decision, only to experience consequences we soon regret. How do you get guidance to make a wise decision, one that will get you to your desired end? It begins with the first ingredient of Solomon's Recipe: Trust in the Lord. If you can trust in God and place that trust into your decision process, appropriate guidance can be received. Solomon's Recipe worked in these situations for people very dear to me. Their stories set the stage to witness Solomon's Recipe taking action in their lives.

THE VOLUNTEER

It was late on a Wednesday afternoon when I answered the phone. The voice on the other end was agitated and panicked, but familiar. It was my friend Jack, a proud US Marine helicopter pilot.

I had met Jack a few years back when I was serving as a minister in our church. Jack introduced me to his wife, Denise, whom he had met and fallen in love with while he was stationed in Florida. Their connection was unique and strong. They married just before Jack was stationed at Marine Corps Air Station Miramar in San Diego.

Jack and Denise regularly attended Sunday morning services. Jack and I "clicked" right away. He was steady, determined, and fiercely loyal. We soon became good friends and shared a deep mutual respect, connecting occasionally for a beer and a burger. On one outing, he shared with me the real danger that he faced as a helicopter pilot: that there was a good chance of not returning once you take off. I made a commitment to support him and pray for him, which only served to deepen our relationship. When he returned home safely from his last deployment, we all heaved a great sigh of relief.

In all our years as friends, I had never heard that sense of urgency in his voice.

"Allan, I'm so sorry to call like this, but I really need some guidance. I think I need you to tell me what to do."

This was not the Jack I had known over the years. He was a man who usually evoked a sense of fearless confidence. I asked him to tell me what was going on.

"Remember a few weeks ago when I told you that my best friend Todd, a helicopter pilot, was shot down in Afghanistan?"

"Yeah, the one who was killed working as a forward air controller. I remember. I've been praying for him and the families of his crew. Why, what's happening now?"

"Well, today my commanding officer informed me that the division is seeking a replacement for him, you know, to finish his mission. They asked me to go, and I just don't know what to say or do. I want to go, I think, and honor my friend. I mean, it's the right thing to do, right? But my wife doesn't want me to. What do I do?"

I knew that the stakes were particularly high, especially now as helicopters in Afghanistan were being shot down way too frequently. I understood why he thought he should go, yet I understood why Denise didn't want her husband to return to the war zone. I found myself in a difficult position. There was no easy answer. In the face of that tough moment, I put my trust in God and silently prayed for guidance before I spoke.

"Jack, I admire your desire to volunteer to honor your friend. I respect you for the willingness to make such a sacrifice. But you must also honor your wife and her desires. The two of you must come to full agreement. I'm sorry, but I can't tell you what to do. However, I will tell you what I would do. This evening is a service at church. I would ask God to provide me with the right answer in the service tonight. I would place this situation in the Lord's hands,

29

trusting that His word for me would come from a minister who knows nothing of my situation. That's what I would do."

I sensed that my answer was not what Jack expected. There was an awkward silence before Jack responded.

Reluctantly he said, "Okay, thank you. I'll talk it over with Denise and decide what to do next."

He hung up the phone.

Jack and Denise did not normally attend services on Wednesdays. Denise had been attending school and Jack's schedule usually didn't allow regular midweek freedom. I prayed, asking God to provide a clear direction for them through the words of the sermon. I also asked that if they didn't attend the service for whatever reason, to please give me their answer.

I asked my wife Carol to pray with me as well. After dinner, Carol and I left for church. I sat in the pew and kept wondering if Jack and Denise would make it. In the quiet before the service, I resisted the temptation to turn around to see if they had come.

The service began, and I was excited to see that the minister conducting the service was new to our congregation. He had just recently been assigned to serve us and didn't know every one of the members, and certainly not Jack and Denise.

As the service progressed, I heard a message that stirred great excitement in my soul. It was a simple message, but precisely focused. I so hoped that they had made it to the service. When it came time for Holy Communion, I noticed they were there. I was thrilled for them, anticipating that they heard the same answer I did.

When the service concluded, I made a beeline to Jack and Denise.

"Wow! Wasn't that an extraordinary sermon?"

Their faces didn't reflect my excitement.

Jack shrugged solemnly. "It was a wonderful sermon, but we didn't hear an answer. Can you talk with us?"

"Of course. Let's go into the Mother's Room for privacy."

We entered the room and closed the door. I looked into their expectant eyes, hoping they would see what I did as I explained the revelation I had heard.

"Here's what I received from the sermon. When faced with a critical decision with no easy solution, place it God's hands through a fervent, heartfelt, believing prayer. Then make the best decision you can. If it is the right decision, God will support it, and all will be well. But if it is the wrong decision, God will change things, and all will be well."

Tears welled up in their eyes, and they hugged each other in relief.

"Will you please pray with us?"

"Well, I actually think you should have the minister that conducted the service pray with you. Would that be okay?"

They agreed and I introduced Jack and Denise to the minister, who stated that he would be honored to pray with them.

The three entered the sacristy and closed the door.

I waited outside the door, anxious to see what would happen next. My purpose in directing them to the other minister was to take myself out of the situation and place it solely in God's hands. Since the minister had no knowledge of what had happened in the previous hours, his prayer and what would follow would be completely in the purview of God. God and only God would gain acknowledgment for the outcome.

A few minutes later, they exited the sacristy and Jack raced out the front door. I feared that something happened that Jack couldn't accept. Although I didn't know it, he had committed to his commander earlier that he would provide an answer by nine o'clock that evening. It was about eight-fifty when Jack rushed out the door. Denise came over to me and I asked her what they decided.

"We decided he's volunteering to go."

"Are you okay with that, Denise?"

"After the understanding from the word in the sermon and the prayer with the minister, we know it is all in God's hands, and we believe He will ensure all goes well."

The next day in the early afternoon, my phone rang. It was Jack. He sounded relieved, elated even.

"Allan, it happened just like you said, just like you said!"

"What happened, Jack?"

"I just left my commanding officer. He thanked me and my crew for volunteering to finish my friend's tour. And then out of nowhere, he said that they had made a different decision on the matter and would not need us to go after all."

I was quietly thrilled and offered up a silent prayer of thanksgiving.

Jack concluded, "Just like you said. We put it into God's hands, made a decision, and He changed it!"

So, in the end, Jack felt good for courageously volunteering, but God ensured that His will and blessing prevailed and Denise's hope was fulfilled.

~

When we begin our work to trust in the Lord, we may start to see the ways in which He will carry us through our toughest moments. Or, maybe when others suffer and question, our trust in the Lord can possibly be a blessing to someone in need.

QUESTIONS to inspire:

Am I willing to trust God when I see no solutions?

Am I willing to commit without complete understanding?

Can I accept that a divine or greater power is at work for me?

Am I grateful for unfolding guidance when I experience it?

Make-A-Wish

Zoey was in her twenty-second week of battling for her life against the ravages of leukemia.

She was eighteen and the daughter of a dear friend, Dawn.

The battle was intense, the side effects of the heavy chemo adding to her pain. Her organs were being attacked from the inside out.

As I walked into the hospital, I thought about how bravely she was facing down this disease. I thought back on an early interaction when she was just three years old.

It was her grandpa's birthday party. She was nestled in his arms when I approached to say hello. I offered her a large smile, but she returned only a frown. With her hands on her hips she called out to me.

"When are you going to come and visit me?" she stated in a commanding voice.

As a minister in our church, I often made family visits.

"But, Zoey," I said, "I have visited you."

She stood her ground firmly and shook her head.

"No! That's not right. You visit us, but you always talk with Mommy and Daddy, and then they send me off to bed. I want you to talk with me and send them off to bed."

I was so taken by this little girl's declaration, I could feel my heart melting. She and I were connected, and she knew it. Smiling, I looked at her and met her eyes.

"Zoey, that's a great idea! I'll talk with your mommy and come to visit you soon."

Later that evening, I arranged with Zoey's mother to visit the following Thursday.

~

When I knocked on the family's apartment door, it opened wide and there stood Zoey, happily waiting to welcome me in.

"I have cookies and milk for our visit. I made the cookies with my grandma today."

I came in, greeted Zoey's parents, and took a seat on the sofa. Zoey sat across the coffee table from me. Just as she had promised, on the table was a glass of milk, a plate of chocolate chip cookies, and a cup of coffee for me. And just as Zoey had wanted, Zoey's parents left for their bedroom, leaving us to have our own visit.

"Zoey, thanks for inviting me to visit with you. You did such a wonderful job preparing. I love chocolate chip cookies, they're my favorite. Before we start, let's pray."

"Okay."

I offered a brief prayer and we talked and shared our thoughts, but I mostly listened to her exciting report of her day with her grandma.

At the end of our visit, Zoey and I prayed again, thanking God for all the blessings we have in our life.

As I walked out of their apartment that day, I was filled with gratitude for the lesson Zoey had taught me—just how important it was to connect with the children in my ministry.

And here I was, fifteen years later, walking down this stark green hallway to visit her in the hospital.

As I approached her room, I thought about the problem her mom had posed to me in an email earlier in the day. She explained to me that a few months back, Zoey's condition reached Make-A-Wish. The Make-A-Wish Foundation is an organization that seeks to bring joy to children facing daunting and life-threatening diseases and injuries. Apprised of Zoey's battle, the foundation asked what her wish would be.

Zoey was an avid fan of the TV show *Lost*. The story was about the challenges faced by the survivors of a plane crash on what seemed to be a deserted island. Zoey was particularly enamored with Michael Emerson, one of the main actors. Her wish was to have tea with him.

Make-A-Wish went to work swiftly, contacting the actor's agents to see if a meeting could be arranged. After some weeks of effort, his agents notified Make-A-Wish that he would like to send a limousine to San Diego and bring Zoey and her parents to Los Angeles for a couple of days. Hotel arrangements would be made and a day that included theme parks and tea was planned.

When Dawn heard about the plan, she was elated; she knew what this day could mean for her daughter. She knew that this could be a bright light in a sea of painful monotony.

Zoey was over the moon. Dawn was holding onto this plan as a lifeline.

After firming up the details, Dawn consulted with the doctor, who offered a harsh blow.

"I'm so sorry, Dawn, but Zoey just isn't strong enough to make a trip like that. We don't think it's a good idea."

"But I've promised her. She is looking forward to it. Just the thought is keeping her going right now."

"I get it, Dawn, I do. But the honest truth is that not only is she not strong enough, but an ordeal like that might just make her condition worse and put her treatment regimen in jeopardy."

And with that news, Dawn faced one of her biggest dilemmas.

Obviously, her first consideration was to keep her daughter on a track for the best chance for recovery. But the cost of depriving Zoey of her wish was almost as troubling.

We had talked earlier in the day as she wrestled with the decision. Emotions rose, lobbying for Zoey's moments of happiness among the long endless days of a battle wrought with pain. Dawn was looking to me for some guidance. She had emailed me, "I am struggling with this decision. If I give permission to go ahead with Zoey leaving the hospital for a few days to go to Los Angeles and fulfill her dream and wish, I could jeopardize her recovery. If I don't let her go, I deprive her of her dream. I just don't know what to do."

As I reached the hospital room, I wondered what guidance I would offer. It was then that my mind went back to the recent experience I had with Jack, the Marine helicopter pilot.

"Dawn, I have learned that when decisions seem to be beyond us, we should pray with a believing and trusting heart. Then trustingly put the decision into God's hands. Afterward, make the best decision you feel from your heart. If it's the right decision, God will give His full support. But if it's the wrong decision, He will change things to ensure you and Zoey are blessed."

Dawn nodded, taking in my words. I held her hand.

"I will pray with you for God's guidance."

Dawn prayed as well, and she trustingly placed it all in the hands of God. Then she made her decision. She called Make-A-Wish and advised them of Zoey's condition. She explained that regretfully Zoey could not accept their generous offer. She asked them to kindly explain this to Michael Emerson's agents, and she expressed her and Zoey's sincere thanks.

It was a painful decision for Dawn to make. Pangs of guilt and disappointment gripped her heart as she watched her daughter struggle mightily against the disease without something to look forward to.

Then, just a few days later, Make-A-Wish contacted Zoey's mother, explaining that they told Michael's agents about the situation.

"Michael wondered, since she could not come to Los Angeles, if he could come down to San Diego."

Dawn asked the doctors if Zoey would be able to have such a visit, and if she could go to a small teahouse near the hospital. The doctors agreed it could work. The next week, Michael Emerson did just that. He drove down to San Diego and they shared an afternoon of tea and laughter. They talked about their love of the TV show and the intricacies of the story. The hours spent together lifted Zoey's spirits and renewed her determination to continue her battle with leukemia.

Dawn was filled with gratitude. Just as we had discussed, by placing the decision in the hands of God, He changed things by touching the heart of Michael Emerson to go out of his way to fulfill the wish of a young woman battling for her life.

Michael was so touched by his experience with Zoey that he remained in contact with her via email for the duration of Zoey's battle.

QUESTIONS to inspire:

Am I willing to trust God when I am unsure and must make a critical decision?

Am I willing to decide when I am torn between options and lack understanding?

Do I accept a divine or greater power's influence working to help me?

When I experience successful guidance from God, am I willing to profess it?

Clara's Story

Carol and I had just finished unpacking from a vacation in Alaska when a call came in from New Jersey. It was Carol's Aunt Helen. She sounded worried.

"Carol, I think you should come and visit your mother. You need to assess her condition. I fear for her safety."

For thirty-eight years after she had been widowed, my mother-in-law Clara lived alone in an upstairs apartment in New Jersey. It was a small one-bedroom flat in the house of her nephew and his family. Her younger sister Helen lived just across the street, so Clara was surrounded by loving and supportive family members. Carol's brother Rudy lived about an hour's drive away from Clara, in Sussex County in northwestern New Jersey. Carol and I lived 2800 miles across the country in San Diego. Once a year, Carol and I would visit Clara and the family in the east coast.

"What's going on, Aunt Helen?"

"It's her short-term memory. She keeps forgetting things. Just yesterday I visited her and found she hadn't eaten her breakfast. She said she forgot. I fear something more serious and dangerous could happen next."

Carol got on the next plane. When she arrived, her worst fears were confirmed. There was cause for alarm. Clara was having trouble doing everyday tasks like making her breakfast, and she was becoming increasingly confused daily.

Something needed to be done, and quickly. Carol and her brother Rudy took Clara in for a thorough medical evaluation. They met with an eldercare professional to get an understanding as to how best to deal with the results of the medical findings. It became very clear that from that point forward, Clara would need to have some level of assistance in her daily life.

Various scenarios were considered. But they finally concluded that the best course of action was to find an assisted living facility. The question was where?

She could stay in New Jersey or we could move Clara close to us in San Diego. While Carol and Rudy investigated details of available facilities in New Jersey, I investigated facilities in the San Diego area. After we had fully looked over all the options, we concluded that the best facility for Clara was only a few miles from us in San Diego.

But that decision posed some challenges.

Clara suffered from claustrophobia, so flying would be a big hurdle. Added to that was the guilt that gripped Carol by taking Clara away from the rest of the family. Carol was under a lot of stress and called me for support.

"Allan, I just don't know what to do. Do I keep Mom here or do I bring her home to San Diego?"

I shared with her what I had learned from my two previous experiences.

I said, "Carol, pray about the decision you need to make. Trustingly and faithfully place it God's hands. Then decide. If it's the right decision, God will bless and support it. If it's the wrong decision, He'll change things."

I assured Carol I would pray for her to be guided to make the best decision.

Carol prayed and handed it over to God. Then she decided to bring her mother to San Diego.

Once the wheels were in motion, everything fell into place. The family helped move Clara's furniture into storage and Carol made special arrangements with Southwest Airlines for the trip to San Diego. The trip went very smoothly, as the airline personnel treated Clara with the utmost care and respect. She never even thought about her claustrophobia and didn't need any medication to counter it. Clara did ask for a glass of wine when the flight attendant inquired if she wanted something to drink.

When Clara arrived at our home, I greeted her.

"Mom, you are welcome to stay with us for as long as you want."

One of Clara's character traits was that she never wanted to put someone out of their normal routine. With this in her mind, it took just a few weeks for her to make her wishes known.

"I really want a place of my own."

That was not surprising, as she cherished her independence.

"Mom, there are several assisted living facilities nearby. We can take you to visit two of them. There's a large one and small one very close by. Let's see which one will make you comfortable and happy."

First, we visited a small facility, the one nearest our home. Then we went to a large luxury facility a few miles further away.

As we were leaving the large facility, Clara said, "This place is nice, but it is so big I would feel lost in here. I want to go to the smaller place."

The stage was set to move Mom to the facility nearest our home, called the Arbors. We met with the staff and made the arrangements. She would have a newly renovated room with a private bathroom. The move date was scheduled, and Carol and I set out to buy the furnishings Clara would need to outfit her room.

The day before the move in, Carol prayed.

"All I ask, Lord, is that my mother finds at least one friend in this place, so if a day comes that I can't visit her, she will have a friend."

The next morning, I went to the facility with the furniture kits we had purchased and the tools to assemble them. While I was busy putting the furniture together, Carol and her girlfriend picked up Mom's bed.

By early afternoon, the room was arranged and ready for Clara's arrival. We returned home, packed Clara's clothes, and headed off to the Arbors. When the manager from the Arbors came in to make sure all was well and to offer her personal welcome, she invited Carol to share dinner that evening with Clara.

Carol remained with her mom into the evening to help her acclimate to her new home. At dinnertime, Carol and Clara enjoyed their first meal together at the Arbors. As the other residents passed by their table, Carol stopped them, saying, "This is my mother, Clara. She's just moved here from New Jersey. This is her first day at the Arbors."

After a few introductions, a lady with a big smile, Dorothy, replied, "I'm from New Jersey too! I lived in Union City."

Carol said, "We lived in Gutenberg, right next door!"

The lady smiled wide. "I worked in Gutenberg at an embroidery factory."

Carol was heartened, adding, "My mother and father worked in an embroidery factory too. It was called Solar-Bell."

Dorothy was struck. "That's where I worked too!"

It soon became clear that seventy years earlier, Clara and Dorothy had worked side by side in that embroidery factory. They had been friends. Now in their nineties and almost 3000 miles away, they were reunited.

When Carol told me this story later that evening, I wrote a report to the local news station. We were contacted by a reporter from the news station the next day, and within a few weeks a meeting was arranged at the Arbors. In the days leading up to the meeting, I obtained from Dorothy some old photos that she had from the days in the factory. I made several copies and had some of the photos enlarged.

The reporter and her cameraman from the news station arrived and we set up for the filming.

Carol, Clara, and Dorothy were arranged around a table with the photos. The reporter asked the three women questions that inspired nostalgic conversation as the camera rolled.

The interview aired on the news a few evenings later. It was such an amazing story, it aired on national TV a day or two after that.

Quickly, social media was abuzz with the tale. The family members in New Jersey were shocked that their Aunt Clara, who lived in New Jersey for almost ninety years and never made a wave, had made national news after less than a month in San Diego!

Carol and I considered this wonderful reunion of two friends as profound evidence that God had blessed Carol's decision to bring her mother to San Diego.

That blessing was further reinforced when just eight months later, Carol's brother passed on from cancer.

QUESTIONS to inspire:

Can I honestly trust God when I can't see a clear path to a solution to my dilemma?

Lacking understanding, am I willing to decide based on my trust in God?

Do I have the courage to accept that a divine or greater power is at work for me?

Do I have the patience to await the evidence that the guidance received was the best solution for me?

Our prayers may be awkward. Our attempts may be feeble. But since the power of prayer is in the One who ears it and not in the one who says it, our prayers do make a difference.
                                        -Max Lucado

Trust in the Lord includes trusting the Lord's timing...

Chapter 2

RELATIONSHIPS

One of the most important aspects of our lives is relationships. How we relate to others is key to how we find our happiness. Solomon's Recipe can have a significant impact on our relationships and how we develop them. We all have our prejudices; some are acknowledged and some lay hidden within us. When we trust God and can follow the inspiring guidance of the Holy Spirit, we will meet some of the most wonderful people and form the most rewarding relationships of our lives.

The Perfect Gift

During my high school years in Garfield, New Jersey, I seldom dated. When I did, I dated because I wanted to take someone to a specific event, like a dance or a party. I had no interest in looking for a wife. I was focused on getting a college education.

In college I had much the same mindset, even though there were many opportunities to date. I enjoyed the company of wonderful young ladies for social events but had no expectations. During the summer between my junior and senior year in college, I took an evening anthropology class. There I met Hanna, a very sweet and smart young lady. At the end of the course, I asked her on a date. We dated for the rest of the summer. I found her to be an extraordinary woman. Her character and my feelings for her caused me to think about looking for my wife.

For the next four years, I met and dated some very special ladies. Although each relationship ended amicably, I was disappointed. They were women of character. Women I thought would be good for me and me for them. Finally, I dated Cheryl, a young lady whom I could not imagine as a spouse. At this point I was ready to give up.

The night that Cheryl and I broke up, October 22, 1967, I went home and wondered, *How am I going to find a wife? What am I doing wrong?* That night I decided to pray and see what God might have in store for me. My prayer was an expression of the realization that my plan to find a true life partner was not working.

I asked, "God, since my plan isn't working, please find me the wife you want for me."

With that, I turned over and went to sleep.

On Sunday morning, I prayed before church.

"Lord, you know I'm looking for a woman with whom I can spend the rest of my life. Someone who is just right for what my future will be. Since I have no idea what my future is going to be, I'm placing this effort into Your hands. Please guide me so that I can recognize the woman You have in store for me."

Nothing happened until I went to church the following Wednesday evening, October 25. At the end of the service, the priest announced that the following Sunday, the highest officiant of our church was going to be conducting a service in Ontario, Canada. The church had chartered a plane scheduled to fly to Ontario's Toronto airport early Sunday morning. The cost was forty dollars per person. I turned around and looked at my friend Mike sitting behind me.

"Mike, are we going?"

He nodded. "Yes, we are!"

Mike and I signed up and paid our forty dollars. I assumed Mike was going to be alone and that we'd sit together on the plane.

The rest of the week I continued my daily prayer to God.

I arrived at the airport Sunday morning and was surprised to see Mike walking hand in hand with his twenty-one-year-old daughter. Suddenly, I found myself feeling very alone. I thought, *What now?* Little did I know, God's plan for me was unfolding before my eyes.

I greeted Mike and his daughter but showed no sign of my surprise or disappointment. I continued my walk alone toward the gate. In the distance I saw a group of members from our North Bergen church, and among them was a strikingly beautiful woman I remembered first meeting when I was fourteen. Her name was Carol Solar and she had been in my confirmation class. The image of her in her stunning white confirmation dress had stayed with me.

I hadn't known her well. I remembered admiring her from afar. My thoughts went back to our days in confirmation class. The few times we were together, I was struck by her beauty but also by her personality. I deemed her to be out of my league. In my humble mind, she was beyond hope for a relationship, confirmed when I noticed her dating older guys.

But over the years, Carol and I became casual friends. All our friends at church our age had already married, so we were the lone singles. Whenever our two congregations gathered together, we would seek each other out and chat about travels or people we knew in common.

That morning at the airport when we saw one another, we greeted each other warmly. I was elated with this unexpected and unplanned meeting with her. *Could this be God's answer to my prayer? Is Carol the one?* I was thrilled, wondering as we sat together for the flight. Our conversation was effortless and before we knew it, we were circling around the Toronto airport.

"I wonder why we are circling," Carol mused out loud.

Just then the pilot came on the PA and announced that the airport was closed, and no planes had landed all morning because a thick fog bank was blanketing the airport.

"We are going to make one more circle and if the fog bank doesn't open, we are going to return to Newark."

We were all disappointed. My cousin Ed Stier, an evangelist in our church and the de facto spiritual leader on the flight, decided it was time to do something. He stood up and we joined him in a prayer. He asked the Lord to please open the fog bank, allowing the plane to land. The moment we offered up a hearty and united "Amen," the pilot came on again.

"Buckle up everyone, we are cleared to land!"

The plane landed, and we deplaned and rushed to a waiting bus. We all boarded and headed toward McMaster University.

It was thirty-nine miles from the Toronto airport. The service was being held in the school gymnasium. Word of our late landing had reached the ministers, so the service had been delayed till we arrived.

When our bus arrived, Carol and I entered the packed gymnasium. To my surprise, we quickly found two perfect seats. Had we been there two or three hours before everyone else, we couldn't have picked better seats.

I knew that Carol didn't feel this way, but I felt my prayers had been answered. Carol was lovely, smart, and beautiful, and I felt that we just clicked. I was convinced the Lord had guided our hearts together.

When the service was over, Carol said she wanted to visit her friends from our church in Holland, Michigan. I said I'd visit my friends from the Los Angeles congregations. We briefly separated, visited our respective friends, and met back at the bus.

The bus returned us to the airport. Throughout our traveling between the airport and the university, Carol and I were wrapped in conversation. Since our flight wasn't going to leave for a few hours, we had time to have lunch at the Aeroquay Restaurant in the airport.

Carol and I sat together with eight friends at a table for ten. We requested separate checks from the waiter. I planned to treat Carol to the late lunch. We ordered cocktails to start. The waiter arrived carrying a tray of a half dozen whiskey sours, but he tripped and fell right behind Carol's chair. The whiskey sours spilled all over Carol's coat and dress. The waiter, Chris, was apologetic and immediately used a towel to wipe up the mess created by his fall.

The excitement over, new drinks were served and soon the meals came to our table. We enjoyed our meal and the conversation with our friends. The waiter returned and gave me our check.

I was surprised, expecting the event with the dress and coat would have caused the restaurant to absorb the check. Reading my mind, Carol whispered to me, "Don't make a scene."

"I won't, but excuse me, I need to go to the restroom."

As I walked, I thought, *That's Carol, always thinking kindly of the other person, considerate especially when they are in difficulty.*

On the way to the restroom I stopped at the maître d's desk and explained the situation with the drinks and the dress and hinted that maybe they could cover the bill. He explained the restaurant's policy for issues such as this.

"No, I'm sorry we can't cover the bill for lunch, but we can reimburse you for the cleaning."

"That's going to be difficult because we're from New Jersey and I don't know what the cleaning is going to cost."

"Well, just make an estimate and I will give you reimbursement."

I looked down at the check. It was eighteen dollars.

"I think it's going to be about twenty dollars."

That was enough to cover the check and tip. I left and went to the restroom. Returning, I walked past his station, and he handed me twenty dollars in cash in Canadian funds and asked me to sign a voucher indicating my receipt of the money. I signed the voucher and returned to our table. I used the money to pay the bill and added a few extra US dollars for the tip. Carol's comment had softened my disappointment at the incident and made me see a more gracious way to view it.

Carol and I boarded the plane and sat together for the journey home. The whole way I subtly attempted to get a date, but she very carefully and diplomatically refused. That was disappointing, considering my growing feelings. I thought, *I'll just have wait to see what happens next*, firmly believing Carol was the woman God was guiding to me.

We arrived in Newark and I bid Carol goodbye. I asked her to please let me know the cost of the bill from the cleaners for her coat and her dress. I said I wanted to reimburse her for the cleaning. I gave her my phone number and we said goodbye and headed home.

That night I prayed and thanked the Lord for His guidance and awaited further developments. My hopes were flying high.

On Monday evening, Carol called. She said she took her dress and coat to the cleaners on her way to work in New York City that morning. On her way home, she picked them up.

"What was the cost?"

"Eighteen dollars."

"I'll put a check in tomorrow's mail."

"Allan, do you remember the name of the restaurant at the airport?"

"Yes, but why do you ask?"

"Well the dress was damaged beyond repair and I was hoping to write a letter to see if I can get reimbursed. It was rather expensive."

I told Carol that I had saved a matchbook with the pertinent information. Then I told her about my conversation with the maître d'.

"Carol, if you write a letter, they have no way to confirm that you were there. They have my name and signature on record. Let me write the letter. How much was the dress?"

"Forty dollars."

"I'll write the letter tomorrow. Are you available Saturday for dinner?"

"No. Sorry. But thank you."

Disappointed again at my failure to get a date, I looked forward to the morning and began composing a letter in my head.

Tuesday morning, I sat at my desk and dictated a letter to my secretary. It was addressed to the president of the Aeroquay Restaurant. I carefully worded the letter, identifying Carol as my "female companion" and wording the letter with diplomacy. I praised the waiter and maître d' for the gracious way they dealt with the incident. I explained in detail the circumstances that prompted the letter and request for reimbursement. The letter stated that the dress cost forty-five dollars, as I considered the exchange rate.

My secretary typed the letter with three carbon copies. We didn't have Xerox machines then, so copies were on very thin tissue paper. The original was sent airmail to Toronto and a carbon copy was sent to Carol.

Wednesday, early in the evening, Carol phoned me. She had just received her copy of my letter. Carol was quite impressed with it.

"Wow Allan, if that letter doesn't get results, I don't think anything will. Thank you."

I seized the moment and asked her again for a date on Saturday night. This time she accepted.

Saturday, we had cocktails and talked. I was attending night school, so every night after that first date, I visited Carol after my classes ended at ten o'clock.

With each hour we spent together, I saw more of the character traits I hoped for in a wife. I became even more convinced that Carol was the one for me.

I planned a special romantic evening three weeks later, for the day after Thanksgiving. I brought Carol to my house and made a fire in the fireplace. I piped Johnny Mathis love songs through the TV speakers. There in front of a crackling fire, with Johnny singing, I took my shot and asked her to marry me.

Carol's answer was simple. To the point. "No."

It was at that moment that I realized there must be another guy in the picture. I was going to have to fight to win her over.

I immediately started to plan to win Carol's heart. My first step was to talk to her mother.

"What has Carol always wanted but never received?"

Her mother thought for a few minutes.

"She has a silver charm bracelet, but she always wanted a gold charm bracelet."

I took my mother to a jewelry store in Passaic, New Jersey, to get her wise perspective. We found a perfect dainty gold charm bracelet. I chose a charm of a fireplace with stockings. It was the perfect Christmas gift for Carol. The plan was complete. I just had to wait for Christmas, three weeks away.

A week later, I called Carol as I always did during my break between classes. Her younger brother Rudy answered the phone as he always did.

"Solar residence, which one of the heavenly bodies would you like to speak to?"

"Carol."

"Oh, ahhh, err, she's not home. Carol is out with the girls."

I knew something was up because she never went out with the girls. I figured she was going out with the other guy.

When we met the next day, Carol told me she broke off with the gentleman she had been dating. He was in the Army and was home from his duty station. Her reason for waiting was that she didn't want to write him a Dear John letter. She wanted to break up with him face to face. This further revealed the depth of her character; confirmation Carol was the one for me. My plan for my next proposal was now in full swing.

During the many evenings we spent together at her parents' home, I saw the deep respect she had for her family. She was always helping her mother when I joined them for Sunday lunches, when they always had several guests at the dinner table. The joyful generosity of this family was not lost on Carol. My respect and love for Carol grew deeper and deeper.

Christmas came, and Carol loved her gold charm bracelet gift. My plan for the next proposal was to propose on Carol's birthday. It had to be something extremely special and very romantic. I discovered there was a unique restaurant in an old gristmill called the Powder Horn Mill Inn. It was built in the late seventeenth century and was owned by two millionaire bachelors. They turned it into a restaurant but did not serve any alcoholic beverages. It was a bring-your-own-alcoholic-drinks policy, to encourage only the most discerning diners. Furthermore, you had to order your food in advance. They bought everything based on their client's personal tastes.

The weather was not cooperating on the Sunday of Carol's birthday. A bitter-cold torrential rain was blanketing northern New Jersey. My plan had to cut through the miserable weather on the twenty-eighth of January, 1968, to make this the special day for Carol. We drove to my parents' house so they could wish Carol a happy birthday. My dad snuck out the back door. He opened the trunk of my car and placed inside an ice bucket with a bottle of champagne. We headed out to the restaurant.

Carol had no clue where we were going. When she asked, I told her it was my surprise. It was a long ride in the cold, rainy night. I turned off the highway onto a narrow country road. A few miles later, I turned onto a gravel tree-lined driveway. Then, there in the darkness of the forest, was the quaint grist mill. Its huge aged wooden waterwheel slowly turned to the splashing of the creek water that powered it. Lights flickered in the windows. It was magical.

I got out of the car, opened an umbrella, and retrieved the bucket of ice and the champagne. I opened Carol's door. We huddled together under the umbrella and walked briskly toward the restaurant. We crossed a little bridge over the stream next to the gristmill's waterwheel and went inside. We received a warm welcome from a waitress dressed in a period floor-length peasant dress. It turned out that we were the only patrons there. Everyone else cancelled due to weather.

We were seated at an antique table with a white tablecloth. A candle in an ornate pewter candleholder sat between us. Filled with antique furniture, it felt like we were dining at a wealthy estate manor. I was thrilled as I peered into Carol's eyes. Her smile told me she was happy. Not far from our table was a grand piano.

It could not have been more romantic.

I had preordered the house specialty, Powder Horn Mill porterhouse steaks and baked potatoes. It was our favorite meal. One of the owners sat at the piano playing love songs. It was all I hoped it would be.

When dinner was over, we left our table for a love seat in front of the fireplace. There we were served coffee and cheesecake. I gave Carol her birthday gift. The small box was neatly wrapped with tissue paper, ribbon, and a tiny bow. Carol smiled and began to open the box. The box revealed a gold heart-shaped charm I had custom made.

I felt the time was perfect and I proposed again. With a sparkle in her eyes, Carol accepted. My dream came true in that moment. My heart was full.

God had given me the perfect gift.

QUESTIONS to inspire:

Can I honestly trust God when all my plans and efforts seem to fail?

When I can't find understanding of the path I am taking, can I remain trusting in God?

Can I maintain confidence that it's God's work for me during ups and downs along the way?

Do I have the patience to await the evidence that the guidance received was the best for me and my future?

What's the Question?

During the time I was an acting minister, a young married couple, Jenny and Paul, pulled me aside after a Sunday service and asked me to pay them a pastoral visit. They shared that they were experiencing some serious difficulties in their marriage. I could see the distress in their eyes. Almost a sense of hopelessness. I agreed to meet them at the end of the week.

The days slowly passed by for me. I was concerned. *What could I contribute to their troubling situation? Was their marriage in serious jeopardy? Would I say the right things?* This thought stirred painfully in my soul. *They have two young children. What effect would a breakup have on them?* I prayed every day for guidance, yet my praying had yielded nothing of substance. I felt empty and ill prepared. I wondered why God had not come to my rescue.

The evening of our meeting arrived, and I prayed as I made my way to their home, butterflies in my stomach. I felt so inadequate as I reached the front door and knocked.

I was welcomed in and led to the living room. Suddenly, an air of confidence came over me, but I didn't understand why.

As we sat down, I noticed how far apart Jenny and Paul sat from one another. It seemed to me that a distance had grown between them. I took a deep breath and began.

"The way I like to proceed is to first pray together, because I need God to be a part of our discussion and an active participant in the solution. We need His guidance because His solution will be successful. After we pray, I would like each of you in turn to share your perspective of the issues and concerns. Then I will work to bring God's perspective to the discussion. We will end with a prayer of thanksgiving."

All agreed. But then I said something that surprised me. It was completely unplanned and never crossed my mind in my days of preparation.

"Whatever the outcome of our discussion, the success or failure will depend on the answer to one question."

Thoughts raced about in my head—*What is that all about? Where did it come from? What's the question? More important, what's the answer?*

Now, ill at ease again, I realized that any sense of confidence had evaporated.

I asked Jenny to share the issues from her perspective. She expressed her feelings articulately. For a good thirty minutes, she went down a laundry list of complaints. Paul didn't help her with childcare. He didn't seem concerned when she had a bad day. He could be insensitive and rude after work.

When Jenny finished, I asked Paul to share his perspectives. He was thoughtful and understanding of his wife's commentary but offered some measures of defense. He was burdened at work, troubled by his demanding boss, and overwhelmed by one of their child's special needs; he tried to do housework but it never seemed to be what Jenny wanted.

When he finished, he leaned forward in his chair.

"So, what's the question?" Paul almost screamed.

Obviously, he had been thinking this during our entire back and forth.

Now I really began to sweat. I didn't know the question. I didn't know the answer. All through the discussion I prayed, asking God the same thing, *What's the question? And what's the answer?*

There was a pause. We sat in silence. I thought it lasted forever. Suddenly I spoke without thinking.

"The question is this: Do you believe it was God who brought you two together? And if you can honestly answer YES, then there is no situation or difficulty that can tear you apart. But if the answer is NO, then the smallest, most insignificant issue can bring your marriage to an end."

No sooner did these words escape my mouth than the couple in spontaneous unison proclaimed, "Yes, we believe God brought us together!"

These words pierced the thick atmosphere in the room. The issues that seemed so insurmountable at the beginning of the evening melted away. Peace returned to this couple and the family that evening.

I told them of my personal concerns and confessed that I had no idea what the question was until I spoke.

We celebrated this gracious gift from God in a prayer of thanksgiving. I saw them look into one another's eyes with softness, even tenderness. Paul reached for Jenny's hand and I left them feeling a deep sense of gratitude.

As I drove home, I realized once more just how much we must be willing servants in His hand, that we can see wonders in how He works when we believe and trust in Him. His guidance sometimes requires us to be ill at ease, uncomfortable, in a place of unknowns. Yet, as the night had proved, when we are in our greatest discomfort, God is at His best! The life of Jesus is a testimony to the Father's mastery at times of human distress.

QUESTIONS to inspire:

Am I still willing to trust God when I am in the heat of a challenging situation?

Do I have the courage to decide, even when there is no understanding or assurance as to what is right?

Accepting that a divine or greater power is at work, can I take the leap and act?

Does the resulting guidance inspire gratitude and encourage professing it as it's experienced?

F-E-A-R
Has two meanings…
Forget Everything and Run
Or
Face Everything and Rise.
The choice is yours.

-Zig Ziglar

Chapter 3

Navigating Life-and-Death Situations

Eventually, everyone reaches a place in life when they must face death. Whether facing one's own death or the death of someone dear to you, the experience is unforgettable. Under these circumstances, Solomon's Recipe can play a crucial part in wending one's way through the emotional and deeply personal journey. As the stories in this chapter will reveal, astounding revelations for ourselves and those we may be positioned to serve will become visible. Wonderful changes to our future perspectives naturally ensue.

Terror on Interstate 5

Dave and I sat in the back seat of a fast-moving car with three strangers we thought had rescued us. It was a cold winter's night in a desolate area of our local interstate. Just a few hours earlier, our car had broken down as we made our way along the empty road.

Any sense of being safe evaporated as the stranger in the front passenger seat bent down to retrieve something. The air all around us turned frigid. Gut-wrenching fear engulfed me. Death was at our door.

It was early in December of 1978. Dave and I, along with two friends, were traveling home following the funeral of a good friend. As we entered the north end of the San Joaquin Valley, a dense fog blanketed the highway. A few cars and tractor-trailers joined us as we all cautiously headed southward. I was driving the first leg of our four-hundred-mile trip home in my friend's diesel Oldsmobile.

Thirty miles into the valley, the engine began to act strangely. I woke my friend next to me and we agreed to stop at the next gas station, but we were unable to get help there. We continued, with him driving.

It wasn't but a half-hour later that the engine seized. We coasted off the road onto the shoulder and then into the dirt. Endless farmland lined both sides of the freeway. The open fields were bordered by barbed-wire fences. Large balls of tumbleweed littered the landscape. It was eerily desolate.

At first, I was not concerned. *Surely someone will stop and give us a ride to the next exit where a tow truck could be called*, I thought.

Standing on the shoulder, we attempted to flag down a few passing cars, but to no avail. It was freezing cold and the fog was growing denser by the minute. As we attempted to flag a few more cars that sped by, we looked at one another with worry. We shared a mutual fear . . .

What are we going to do if no one stops?

We decided three of us would return to the car with just one of us doing the flagging. Within a few minutes, a light-blue Monte Carlo came screeching to a halt, bypassing our position by a good thirty yards. It kicked up a huge cloud of dust.

The car backed up and stopped adjacent to our car. We heaved a sigh of relief. Someone had stopped to help. Three young clean-cut men emerged from the Monte Carlo. They greeted us, offering to fix our car. We told them the engine had seized, so fixing was not an option. We really needed a tow truck. They offered to take one of us to the next exit to make that call. I volunteered to go, since I had towing privileges on my AAA card. Dave volunteered to join me.

The Monte Carlo was a two-door coupe. One man entered the back seat, followed by me in the middle and Dave behind the front passenger's seat, and we drove off. Based on the appearance of the three young strangers, I thought they might be basketball players from nearby Fresno State University.

After a short attempt to make conversation, I quickly realized that they were not interested in engaging. Suddenly the atmosphere in the car changed; it was ominous. A feeling of dread pierced my soul. I watched as the man in the front passenger seat bent down and came up holding a double-barrel sawed-off shotgun. Swiftly, he swung it around, placing the barrels inches from my face.

"This is a stickup!"

As I looked down the barrels of that gun, I realized in those few moments that my life was about to end. In that instant all I thought of was my wife, my son, and my family. I silently prayed as I wondered what God was doing.

Images—thoughts—flashed through my mind.

I was blessed with a loving wife and a precious little boy. We had just settled into my wife's dream house. I had a long-sought-after red sports car. I had a job that was perfect for me. I was also blessed to be serving as a minister in a small local mission. My parents had just moved from the east coast to be with us in San Diego. Every summer we enjoyed a two-week vacation at a beach house just a few miles north of Rosarita Beach in Baja California, Mexico, where I could teach my son the art of fishing.

And all of that could end in less than a minute.

Intense fear seized my soul.

I silently asked, *Is this all You want of me, God? Or is there more You want me to do?*

The gunman seemed to be nervous, his grip shaking ever so slightly. I feared his shaking would set off the gun unintentionally. I thought my words might calm him, so, nervously, I began to speak.

"My name is Allan. You don't have to do this. Is there a way we can talk this through?"

It wasn't working. In fact, my words seemed to anger the driver, who immediately slammed on his brakes. The car skidded off the road, sliding across the shoulder into the dirt in another cloud of dust. As soon as the car came to a stop, the driver turned toward me, his face contorted in a vicious grimace. He grabbed my throat, pushed me up against the rear window, and screamed. "If you don't shut up, we will kill you right now!"

I immediately acquiesced and said, "Okay."

The driver demanded we give them all our money, including our wallets, keys, and watches. I quickly handed everything over but hesitated when handing over my key chain with irreplaceable sentimental attachments. The gold key chain contained my wife's high school ring, a small gold knife, and gifts for being best man at two weddings.

The key chain and knife were gifts for being best man at two weddings.

I wondered how I would explain it to her.

The man next to me collected all we had and proceeded to count the cash. The driver warned us, "If you don't have enough cash, you're going to be shot!"

The man next to me said, "It's only sixty-five dollars."

That was not nearly enough, according to the driver. The gunman opened his door and got out. He stood at the open door, shotgun in hand, and commanded us to get out.

"Walk to the barbed-wire fence. Don't look back. You don't want to know when the shots are fired."

Slowly, Dave got out of the car. He took a few steps toward the fence just a few yards away. As I followed him, I noticed the gunman behind the door; the shotgun was pointed down. When my feet hit the ground, Dave bolted toward the back of the car. Instantly I followed. We ran as fast as we could, hurdling over the three- and four-foot balls of tumbleweed littering the area.

The air, cold and humid, felt like breathing razorblades. My heart pounded. Running for my life, I feared the blast of the shotgun with every step. But it never came. After about thirty yards, hurdling over one tumbleweed after another, I tripped over a large one and fell to the ground. Cautiously, I peered back toward the car through the tumbleweed. I saw the gunman break open his shotgun, pull out two shells, and toss them into the front seat. He jumped into the car and it sped off, leaving a huge cloud of dust and fog.

Dave and I quickly regrouped and attempted to flag down a driver. Within minutes, a car pulled over and the driver offered us a ride. I told him we had just been robbed and needed to call the police and get a tow truck for our friends who were still stranded. The driver said there was a Denny's restaurant a few miles further south.

We arrived at the Lost Hills exit and proceeded to the restaurant. We quickly entered the nearly empty but warm restaurant. It was now one in the morning. A waitress came to serve us. We explained what had happened and she brought us a phone to call the police. We called the police and gave the officer our report. He said it would take him thirty minutes to reach us. The waitress arrived with a burly tattooed man as I hung up the phone, and she said, "Here's Brett, your tow truck driver. He'll take good care of you."

We filled Brett in on the situation and gave him an approximate location of the disabled car and our two friends. He assured us he would find them and return to pick us up. We ordered a cup of coffee and waited.

The police officer arrived shortly, took our statement, and quickly left to pursue the perpetrators. Brett and his tow truck retrieved the disabled car and our friends, then picked up Dave and me at Denny's and drove us all to a nearby car dealership. At dawn we left the car for repairs, got a rental car, and headed home to San Diego.

On the way home, we listened to the radio reporting a high-speed chase down I-5, following three hijackers. After a long pursuit, the three men were apprehended and arrested. Eventually they were all sent to prison for nine years.

When my belongings were returned, I got my wallet, wristwatch, and cash. But missing was my gold key chain. Gone were the gifts for being best man. The loss most painful was my wife's high school ring.

What I realized that very moment was the importance I had placed on material things. I got it. None of that mattered.

By losing what I valued most, I received a more precious gift: the profound realization how foolish it is to place value on *anything* material. I learned to value the people I love and cherish; they are invaluable and irreplaceable. I never underestimate what they mean to me nor do I limit my love for them.

Reflecting, I reached out to God and put myself in His hands. I was preserved and, in the process, delivered a life-changing lesson. From that moment on, I have lived on grace-given time. Every day is precious, appreciated, and lived to the fullest. Each morning I wake up and thank God for the light of yet another day and for the family and people I love. God's grace makes all my days possible.

QUESTIONS to inspire:

Facing death, am I willing to trust God?

Am I willing to decide, when the heat is on and I don't understand what is happening?

Can I still believe that a divine or greater power is there to help me?

Is the guidance received worthy of my gratitude and profession?

At Death's Door

[F]or the Holy Spirit will give you the right words
even as you are standing there. – Luke 12:12, The
Living Bible (TLB)

What can a minister say to a dying soul? How does he know what may be troubling them? Do they suffer from guilt or fear? What do you say to a deathbed confession? How do you comfort them? Indeed, how do you serve them with substance?

I had served in the ministry of our church for thirty-six years and had never been in this situation.

In 2007, I was responsible for caring for two congregations in the San Diego area when I was given the mission of caring for a third congregation in Anaheim. After a few months serving in Anaheim one Sunday a month, I wanted to grow closer to the people. I planned to serve them on a Wednesday evening.

The day prior to my scheduled visit, I received a phone call from the priest in Anaheim. He told me that a church member, Harold Haase, was in a nearby hospital and near death. I heard Harold had not attended church services and was estranged from his family since age eighteen. The priest asked if I would seize the opportunity to visit this man prior to the evening service. When I heard his name, I was moved to answer yes. I had known this man's family since my childhood, though I had never met him. The Haase family came from my hometown, Garfield, New Jersey. Considering Harold was seventy-nine, I assumed he knew my parents.

Driving north to Anaheim, I wondered what to expect. I silently prayed that in some way I could be a blessing for him, and that my visit would make a difference at the end of his life. I wondered, *What could have caused him to leave the church so many years before? What could have estranged him from his family?*

I arrived at the hospital, parked my car, and prayed again.

After my prayer, I made my way to Harold's room. Walking down the corridor, a deep concern filled me as I reconsidered Harold's plight. I entered the room clad in my normal serving attire: a black suit, white shirt, and black tie. I greeted Harold like a long-lost friend.

"Harold! It's so good to see you."

He looked at me in surprise.

"Who are you?"

"I am Allan Musterer."

Quickly and excitedly he responded, "Musterer? Musterer? Sampson Street, Garfield, New Jersey, Musterer?"

"Yes, I am Eddie's eldest son."

"You're Eddie's son! What are you doing here?"

"I am a minister in the New Apostolic Church. Since you are a member of the spiritual family, I'm here to visit you."

Harold sat up in his bed, glared at me with eyes wide open, and forcefully responded.

"Let me tell you why I don't come to church and haven't for years."

With that heated pronouncement, I gave Harold my full attention.

"When I was eight years old, we lived in Garfield on Sampson Street like most of our church families, including many of your family. My

73

brothers and I often played at the Pump House. One Saturday, my brothers and I were playing at the pond when two bullies came by and started hassling us. One of them started pushing me around and ended up shoving me into the deepest end of the pond. I couldn't swim, so I floundered and slipped under the water twice. Gripped in fear of death as I went under the second time, I believed I would never come up again. I was about to die."

As Harold told his story, I found myself feeling very close to him. A deep sense of empathy came over me. As a boy, I lived just a few blocks away from Harold's home and played at the Pump House, the nickname given to the pond just across the railroad tracks at the end of our street. As he spoke, I felt I was there with him.

"Since none of us could swim, it was fortunate there was an adult nearby who saw that I was drowning and ran to my rescue. He pulled me from the water and saved my life. Wet, cold, and dirty, I shook, trembling in fear as my brothers surrounded me. My rescuer urged me to hurry home immediately, so I could get clean and dry. Rattled by my near-death trauma, I ran home, with my brothers right behind me. As I neared home I thought, 'When I get home, my mother is going to be so happy that I didn't drown, she's going to welcome me with open arms and a big hug.'"

I knew Harold's parents were more financially endowed than the other church members. They were a joyfully generous family and every week invited families from church for Saturday dinner and Sunday lunch. Such was the case this Saturday. Harold's mother was busily preparing Saturday's dinner in the kitchen when her boys came barreling into the house.

Harold continued: "I reached home buoyed with high expectations of my mother's warm welcome. To my great surprise, when my mother saw me all wet and dirty, she angrily scolded me and sent me to the bathroom to bathe and get dressed. She said, 'Don't you realize we are having guests for dinner very soon and there's much work yet to be done?' Without another word she went back to work in the kitchen. I was shattered. I felt unloved. I blamed my mother for not hugging me and welcoming me home. I blamed the church because my mother seemed to love the members more than me. I made up my mind that as soon as I was old enough, I was leaving this family and the church behind and going alone into the world."

As Harold was finishing his story, his hurt and pain gripped me. I trembled inside, feeling so inadequate. *What could I possibly say to this man facing death?* I was helpless. I didn't know what to say or where to begin. I silently prayed, *Dear God, please give me something positive to say to Harold. Give something of substance, considering his traumatic experience and near-term death.*

Harold concluded that in his thirties, after some counseling, he reconciled with his mother. But he remained estranged from faith and family. His story finished, he was exhausted. He had poured out his heart, possibly for the last time. He looked at me expectantly through tearful eyes. In response, I began speaking words strange to me, for I spoke of things I did not know, like someone else was speaking through my lips.

"Harold! Consider this: For your whole adult life, you have been a continuous provider of joyfully generous help for people in need. When you saw someone out of work, you gave them a job. When you saw someone living with their family in a car, you put them into a motel till they regained their footing. When you saw someone about to lose their house, you made the mortgage payment. They all were in dire need of work, money, health, and encouragement. Strangers came into your life with needs, and you stepped up graciously and effectively fulfilled them! The pain of your disappointment in childhood created a heart of extraordinary sensitivity and generous charity. You became what your mother and father lived! What a wonderful example your life has become! To all those people, you were and remain a treasured blessing."

Harold sat up in bed, eyes wide open, mouth agape. As he digested what I had said, he sat there, speechless. Once he had collected his thoughts, he looked at me with this *aha!* moment of realization on his face.

"Wow!" he exclaimed, "I never saw it that way!"

The tears rolled down his face. I stood there shocked at what I had just said. I had such little knowledge of his life. The look on his face prompted my silent heartfelt acknowledgment and thanks to God, for it had to be God and His Spirit who supplied the words I spoke. The effect on Harold was undeniable. He suddenly seemed a different man, no longer bound by the anger that held him all those years. I seized this moment to speak.

"Harold, would you like to pray together? We can ask God for His forgiveness and blessing."

"Really? We can do that?"

"Yes, absolutely we can."

Graciously he accepted my offer. I prayed a short prayer and then together Harold and I prayed the Lord's Prayer. I pronounced absolution and we shared Holy Communion. I offered up another prayer and thanked God for the experience we shared. After a tearful goodbye, I left for church.

On the drive home after church, I pondered what had transpired with Harold in that hospital room. I felt honored to have been used by God to bring peace and comfort to an amazing soul who carried a cross of misunderstanding for so many years. I was awed by how, despite his inner pain, Harold had found profound goodness to graciously share with strangers who had entered his life with needs he could fulfill. And to think he did such good works and thought nothing of it.

A few days later, the priest from Anaheim visited Harold. He asked the priest to conduct his funeral service. Shortly thereafter, Harold passed on. Following the funeral, the priest called me with an amazing story. He said that at Harold's funeral service, all manner of people who attended shared their own story of how Harold had saved them from tragic circumstances. The details matched the ones I mentioned that Wednesday in Harold's hospital room.

Yes, "for the Holy Spirit will give you the right words even as you are standing there" became a reality for me.

QUESTIONS to inspire:

When I find myself in an unexpected and unprepared-for situation, can I trust God to rescue me?

Can I make decisions even when I have no clue what is happening in the moment?

Does it become obvious that God is at work with me for a solution?

When the needed guidance takes its course through my action and its perfect result is seen, do I acknowledge it with gratitude and profession?

Losing Joy

Our neighborhood in Garfield, New Jersey, comprised a hundred middle-class families. We were very close, especially to the Colacinos. My brother Roy and I were playmates with Joy and her siblings. In fact, I called Joy Colacino's mom and dad Aunt and Uncle. Roy, who was just five, and I often ran over to their home to watch television. They had the first TV on the block. For a nine-year-old in the 1950s, this was a big deal.

One Saturday, Roy and I attended Joy's tenth birthday party. Joy and I had been best friends since we were three. It was a wonderful party filled with cake, presents, and games, but later that night, Joy became sick. We checked on her on Sunday and found out that whatever was afflicting her just seemed to get worse. By Monday morning, she was too sick to go to school with us.

At lunchtime, my brother Roy and I were walking home from school as we did every day. When we turned the corner onto our street, there it was—a bright red ambulance with red lights flashing, parked in front of our neighbors' house. *Oh no!* I thought.

"Allan, what's going on?" Roy asked me.

"I don't know. Somebody at the Colacinos' house must be very sick. Maybe it's their grandma."

We ran home and asked my mother, "What's wrong?"

"Joy is very sick. She can't breathe. They are taking her to the hospital. Let's pray for her."

The three of us huddled together as my mother prayed. Then we went to the front window and watched as the stretcher bearing Joy's limp body was taken from the house and placed into the ambulance. Fear gripped me. I loved Joy, my friend since I could remember. *Please dear God, help her get well!*

Lights flashing and sirens wailing, the ambulance raced off down the street.

It was hard to eat my lunch. A lump sat in my throat. Oh, how I hoped she would be okay. I nibbled at my lunch until it was time to go back to school. I really didn't want to go, but Mother insisted.

On Monday evening, we all sat around the dinner table. I could tell that something wasn't right. Mother and Dad were speaking low and hushed and in German (as they often did when they didn't want us to know what they were talking about). My brother and I looked at each other, wondering what was happening. *Was it something to do with Joy?* Mother's lip's quivered, betraying her emotions.

When dinner was over, Mother told us the terrible news.

"Joy has polio. It's the kind that attacked her lungs. She can't breathe. They have her in an iron lung to help her to breathe."

This was devastating news for me. I knew polio was a bad disease. Many children were afflicted and couldn't walk without heavy metal braces on their legs and crutches. I knew there was no cure and no vaccine. But I never knew it could affect the lungs.

In the 1950s, polio was a very serious disease and considered highly contagious. When polio compromised a victim's lungs, they were placed in an iron lung. No device was more associated with polio than the iron lung, a tank respirator. Physicians who treated people in the acute, early stage of polio saw patients unable to breathe. The virus's action paralyzed muscle groups in the chest. Death was frequent at this stage.

Joy's prognosis was dire. I knew it was serious because my parents prayed often and intensely for Joy. She remained alive with the iron lung for weeks. Her parents practically lived at the hospital, watching over her. My mother supported Grandma Colacino, who was taking care of Joy's brother and sister, bringing food and words of encouragement as best she could.

During Joy's stay in the hospital, the medical bills for the family mounted drastically. My father and "Daddy" Greiner (our neighbor who earned the nickname "Daddy" because he was so big) walked around the neighborhood with a large brown paper shopping bag. They stopped at each of the one hundred homes in the neighborhood, seeking donations. They were able to amass over $12,000. Considering that this was a blue-collar neighborhood, this was an extraordinary outpouring of love.

~

Despite the prayers of our family and the neighbors for her recovery, and the efforts of the doctors and the iron lung, Joy passed on. I was shattered. I didn't understand. I lost my best friend. Totally bereft, I looked to God.

Then, in the depth of despair, a memory visited me that offered a small amount of inner peace. I thought back on a day that had transformed my view of death.

My Aunt Frieda, my mother's elder sister, had been like a grandmother to me. She always took me on adventures, like rides on buses and trains. So, when she died suddenly when I was just four years old, I experienced a sense of deep loss for the very first time. Seeing my pain, my parents did something that took courage. Despite the traditional thinking at the time, they took me to her wake and funeral.

I remembered entering the funeral home. I was deeply moved by the scene. Huge fragrant flower arrangements (from my small stature) seemed to engulf the whole room like a blanket. The flowers appeared to reach to the sky. Their aroma filled the room. My dad lifted me up so I could see my beloved aunt lying peacefully in the casket, embraced by the sea of flowers.

In that moment, I was given a long-lasting gift: a comforting view of death. In my heart I felt my aunt was at peace.

~

The conditions of the quarantine required that Joy's casket be sealed with a glass cover, and children were not allowed to come to the wake or the funeral. Since my parents were attending the funeral, our neighbor took care of my brother and me. To honor Joy, the funeral procession was scheduled to pass by our school. Because my brother and I were still under quarantine, our neighbor took us to stand across the street from the school so we could witness the funeral procession. We saw all our classmates lining the curb in front of the school. Neighbors lined our side of the street. Then a somber procession of black vehicles, with headlights glowing, slowly made their way down the street.

As the large black hearse carrying my Joy slowly passed, I was filled with the pain of a goodbye I didn't quite know how to say. Tears threatened to consume me. And then, a different sensation poured over me. One of comfort. One of knowing. For somehow my nine-year-old self understood that Joy was truly at peace.

QUESTIONS to inspire:

Am I willing to trust God in the valley of grief and loss?

Can I seek and accept God's comforting actions even without understanding?

When I feel a difference, do I see divine power at work for me?

Do I respond with renewed strength when the help I received is experienced?

You're going to go through tough times-that's life. But I say, "Nothing happens to you, it happens for you." See the positive in negative events. ~Joel Osteen

Sometimes the answer is in your past...

Everything comes to you in the right moment... Be patient.

Every problem has in it the seeds of its own solution. If you don't have any problems, you don't get any seeds. ~ Norman Vincent Peale

Chapter 4

Personal Growth

Those moments when we are thrust into scary and difficult situations open the door for our personal growth. Personal growth stagnates when we can remain in a cozy and secure place. We do not need to face our fears and underestimated view of ourselves and our talent and capabilities. We are fortunate when something enters our safe space and disrupts the status quo. It forces us to reach and grow in the understanding of our true abilities. The stories that follow will reveal how old false perspectives can be whisked away when comfort zones collapse and divine guidance kicks in.

LOSING AND FINDING
THE PERFECT JOB

It was a typical Monday morning. I sat at my desk with my morning cup of coffee and slice of lemon pound cake. Usually the first one in the office, I was prepping for another exciting day. It was 1978 and my life was good. I loved my job. We had just moved to a new house and our beloved son was four years old. And I drove my dream car, a red Triumph Spitfire convertible. I had my California Professional Engineer license that made me indispensable, or so I thought.

My boss walked in earlier than expected and stopped at my desk with a strange look on his face.

"Allan, come to my office," he said with unusual curtness.

I left my coffee and cake behind and followed him down the hall to his office.

He gazed at me across the desk, struggling to form words.

"Last night at 5:15, the company was sold. The new owner is abolishing the engineering department, effective immediately. I bargained with him to give you and your staff until Friday. I'm sorry."

Secretly, I had harbored a dread about losing my job. It was something I never spoke of. This dread, lurking in me, had been sapping my strength and peace of mind, no matter how hard I had tried to hide it.

Standing in front of my boss, hearing the painful news, I found myself responding matter-of-factly.

"Oh, okay. I'll advise the staff when they arrive."

My boss was shocked at my response.

"Allan, are you sure you heard me? You are fired."

"Yes, I understand."

"How can you just take the news in stride like that?"

"If I told you, I don't think you would understand."

~

The day before, a Sunday in February 1978, I had served as a minister in our Vista church for the five o'clock service. Something strange had occurred fifteen minutes into the sermon. I saw what I thought to be an apparition: a piece of paper hovering above the open Bible. This unexpected happening took me by surprise. I continued to speak, but simultaneously I prayed, asking God, "What should I do?"

Prompted by a feeling, I looked down and began to read aloud the words that were now in bold print.

They seemed to jump off the page.

I read, "***In sorrow and grief, heartache and pain, disappointment and injustice, God prepares us for our future.***"

As I read these words, I thought, *Wow, what encouraging words—* for one of the elderly widows in the congregation. She was humble and kind but suffered a hard life with a severely handicapped son and ungrateful neighbors who sought to take advantage of her. *These words can hopefully provide her with some measure of comfort and strength.*

I continued the sermon and greeted the members after the final hymn was sung. No one made mention of these words I had spoken. They obviously fit nicely into the sermon, although I could not tell, as I was too deeply engrossed in the experience.

On the way home that evening after the service, I prayed in thanksgiving to my God for allowing me to be a blessing and convey these special words out of heaven to this widow. When I arrived home, I shared this extraordinary experience with my wife, Carol.

What I didn't understand was the hidden purpose to these words. The unknown mystery was now solved with the words I heard earlier, "YOU ARE FIRED!"

I could once again see those bold words that seemed to jump off the page.

"In sorrow and grief, in heartache and pain, in disappointment and injustice, God prepares us for our future."

Buoyed by these words, I instantly realized they were meant for me.

I called Carol and told her what had happened. I assured her that I would have a new job within a week. She took the news with a sense of calm and understanding.

A moment later, I called Carol again to be sure she was okay with the unexpected turn of events. Alas, the phone was busy. I waited another minute and tried again, but still the line was busy. I phoned my parents, who lived just around the block from our house.

My mother answered.

"Allan, I can't talk—your son just fell off a chair and broke his arm. Dad and I are driving over to take them to the emergency room."

I phoned Carol again and heard Randy screaming in the background.

"What happened?"

"Randy fell off the kitchen chair and broke his arm!"

"How do you know it's broken?"

"He's laying here with his arm bent in the wrong direction and screaming in pain."

"I'm coming right home."

"No, your parents are coming to take us to emergency. I'll call you from there."

I hung up the phone and immediately left my desk for someplace private to pray. I asked God to provide a doctor to care for Randy as we didn't have an orthopedic doctor that we knew. I returned to my desk.

The time had come for me to give my staff the disappointing news. I told them I would provide each of them with a well-earned glowing letter of recommendation.

Back at my desk, my mind was a whirlwind. Big things were happening at the speed of light. But my deep trust in God was strengthened by the words I had spoken the evening before in church. I believed God had something special in store for me and my family. Expecting God's quick action, I took the morning newspaper and scoured it for ads for mechanical engineers. There were none.

Cracks began to form in my confidence.

My phone rang. It was a competing company just down the street. The engineering manager was offering me a job. Obviously, the word of our termination was out on the street.

"We are prepared to offer you a position as a mechanical engineer at ten percent below your current salary. If you are open to it, you can start next Monday," he said.

I asked him if he would give me until the end of the day to consider his offer, and he agreed.

With this turn of events, I felt perplexed and wondered, *Is this God blessing me so quickly? Or is this a test of sorts, keeping me from the real job God has prepared for me?*

I began to pray. A feeling overcame me that led me to believe that I was worth what I was being paid; in fact, I was scheduled to get a raise in the near future. I called the manager back and turned down the job, expressing disappointment in their financial offer. They didn't go any higher.

I decided I needed to get to the hospital to support my family, so I left. At the hospital, our son was examined by the doctor and an x-ray revealed the break.

"This is a serious fracture. I am hoping we can solve it with a cast. I'll be back shortly, and we will get it set. I'll need to take another x-ray in a couple of weeks."

An hour later, Randy's arm was in a cast from elbow to wrist, and we returned home.

Once home, we dealt with our mixed emotions. We were grateful that Randy would be okay, but we were still concerned about my finding a new job.

For the rest of the week, I searched the want ads. Each day that the search came up empty, confidence in God's plan eroded. I rewrote my resume and contacted some employment agencies, but they had nothing positive to offer. My confidence was diminishing with each new setback. Time was running out and the horizon looked dim.

Friday finally came— the day of reckoning. My last day at this, my perfect job, and no new job in sight. I wondered, *Was God going to test me more? Was He going to step in at the last minute?*

At the office, I opened the newspaper again. There it was, tucked in the corner of one of the want-ads pages:

MECHANICAL ENGINEER
IRT Corp.
Send your resume to
7650 Convoy Court, SD.

I looked up the company in the phone book and called. The receptionist answered the phone.

"IRT Corporation. How can I assist you?"

"Hello, my name is Allan Musterer. I am answering the ad for a mechanical engineer. I want to come in for an interview at one o'clock today, please."

"Oh sir, we don't work that way. You need to send in your resume, then we will contact you."

"I understand, but I want to come in this afternoon for an interview. I'll have my resume with me," I said insistently.

"But we don't work that way."

"Please, I want to come in today for an interview," I said with even greater insistence.

Now I am wondering, *What are you doing, Allan? This is not you! You never act this way. You are going to destroy any chance at this job.*

"Sir, please hold the line."

Moments later, another lady came on the phone.

"Hello, my name is Shirley, I am the HR director. How can I help you?"

"Hello, my name is Allan Musterer. I am answering the ad for a mechanical engineer. I want to come in for an interview at one o'clock today."

"I'm sorry, but we don't work that way."

"Yes, I know, your receptionist made that abundantly clear. But I need to come in today for an interview. I have my resume with me."

The sound of my voice revealed a heightened level of insistence and urgency.

"Just a minute; I'll be right back."

"Okay."

"Hello. Can you come in at one o'clock for an interview?"

"Yes. I'll be there at twelve-thirty, so I can complete your employment application."

"Fine, but we don't work that way."

I hung up the phone. Confidence in God's plan took a sudden leap forward. I prepared to leave the office for the final time. I made my rounds, saying goodbye to all my coworkers. With enthusiastic expectations, I jumped into my Spitfire and headed to IRT's offices. I trusted this was God's choice for me. Still, I wondered, *Why was I so forceful?* That just wasn't me. I was way outside the lines of my personality.

I arrived at IRT at twelve-thirty, resume in hand, and walked up to the receptionist. She smiled and handed me a clipboard with the employment application. I finished filling it out just in time to be ushered to the office of the engineering and manufacturing manager, Mr. Clem Pepper.

Mr. Pepper interviewed me for about an hour. We discussed my current position and duties. He seemed impressed and asked me if I could come in for more interviews on Monday.

"Yes, what time would you like me to be here?"

"Can you be here at eight in the morning?"

"I can be here at six if you like."

"Okay, be here Monday morning at seven."

I spent the weekend wondering what would happen on Monday morning. Mr. Pepper had told me that the division of the company he worked in was composed of several PhD nuclear physicists, each running a little "company" of their own. On Monday, I would be interviewed by most if not all of them.

Monday morning, I arrived a few minutes before seven. Mr. Pepper met me in the lobby, gave me a visitor's badge, and escorted me to my first of several interviews with the physicists. My last interview was with the vice president. By the end of the final interview, it was approaching noon. Mr. Pepper took me to a local restaurant for lunch.

At lunch we discussed what salary I wanted. I explained that I was due for an increase and hoped to get between nine and ten percent. We discussed a few other technicalities, but mostly we got to know each other. He was an electrical engineer, so his background complemented my mechanical experience.

He said he would get back to me soon. I went home and shared my experience with Carol, expressing my optimism. I was convinced this was God's handiwork.

Along with all the other things that seemed to go wrong the week prior, our television had died. My dad came to our house after my interviews and we took the TV apart, extracted a dozen vacuum tubes, and headed off to the local drug store where there was a vacuum tube tester.

Dad and I settled in at the tester with a shoebox of tubes. We began testing one tube after another. Before we finished, there was an announcement over the PA system:

"Allan Musterer, please come to the checkout stand, you have a phone call."

I ran to the nearest check stand and answered the phone. It was Carol, telling me to hurry home. Mr. Pepper had called and wanted me to call him back as soon as possible. Dad and I packed up our tubes and raced home.

I made the call to Mr. Pepper.

"Allan, I am pleased to offer you the position of staff mechanical engineer at a salary increase of twelve percent."

"Thank you, Mr. Pepper, I am honored and accept your offer."

"When can you start?"

"What about tomorrow?"

"Wonderful. I will see you tomorrow at eight in the morning."

Carol, Dad, and I rejoiced at this great news. We prayed and thanked God for His guidance that led to this outcome.

I started working at IRT the next day and remained with them for ten years. Along the way were many lessons. A week after I started, Mr. Pepper, now known as Pep, told me that on the Friday he interviewed me, he had previously interviewed another engineer. He had just folded an offer letter to him and put it in an envelope to mail that afternoon. But after our interview, he tore it up in the hope of hiring me.

This information provided the reason behind my acting so pushy. Had I waited to follow the company policy, the job would have been gone.

A couple of months passed, and I was summoned to the president's office. I had no idea why. When I walked in, the president was sitting behind his desk and Pep and our vice president sat on a sofa.

The president observed my discomfort.

"Allan, you don't know why you are here?"

"No, I don't, sir."

"Well, in my long career, this is something I have never seen. Your boss, Pep, has come to me and says that he would rather work for you than you work for him."

I took a long minute to process what I just heard. Before I could speak, the president broke the awkward silence.

"And by the way, Pep is counting on you to keep him on."

"I am honored to accept this promotion and I will do my best to manage these two departments to the best of my ability. And I can assure Pep that he will be here as long as I am."

This job was the most fulfilling work of my career. I was able to perform for ten years under challenging but rewarding conditions. The work required a combination of all my previous professional engineering experiences. The notion that "each job experience prepares you for your future jobs" was fully borne out at IRT for me.

QUESTIONS to inspire:

Am I willing to trust God when everything is falling apart around me?

Am I willing to act outside my comfort, while lacking any understanding?

Can I believe a divine or greater power is at work for me behind the scenes?

When I experience successful guidance from God, am I willing to profess it?

It Doesn't Work—Fix It

It was early 1966 when I was assigned to a power plant nestled on the banks of the Hudson River in Orange County, New York. I was twenty-two years old and on the tail end of a nine-month training program that had taken me to power plants in Pasadena, California, and Las Vegas, Nevada.

I arrived at the plant on a dreary Monday morning. Our team of six engineers met in the cramped company trailer office. Pete, the senior service engineer, handed out the day's assignments to the other engineers, and everyone left to tackle their jobs. I wondered what my assignment would be.

Pete grabbed a drawing from the drafting table. He rolled it up, put it under his arm, and headed for the door.

"Allan, come with me. I have a job for you." My gut sank. *What could he want me to do by myself? What's on that drawing?*

We were met with a waft of cold air as we walked across the muddy area between the trailer and the plant. The wind that came off the river was raw and biting. My sense of foreboding grew. This had all the earmarks of a solo task. I worried that he would ask me to do something I wouldn't be able to do. He was going to figure out where I was weak.

We reached a door that led to the turbine deck. We traversed the turbine deck of the plant and went up the stairs to the burner deck. The foreboding grew as Pete opened the large doors of an electrical panel that housed the control for the automatic coal burner ignition system.

We stood eye to eye as Pete handed me the rolled-up drawing and pointed to the electrical panel. And then he said the words I would never forget.

"This system doesn't work—fix it."

And with that, he turned and walked away. Foreboding was gone. Now it was shock. And dread. What was my biggest weakness? Anything electrical.

I was suddenly seven years old and sitting with my father as he was fixing our broken TV. I was playing with a pair of pruning shears. A long extension cord sat next to me. I did what any seven-year-old would do. I took the pruning shears and cut the extension cord. Instantly a loud crackle split the silence as a massive wave of sparks flew into the air and I was forced up against the wall. The moment was a jumbled mess of my father yelling as I stood frozen in terror.

The sound of the plant brought me back to the moment. I sat on a wooden crate, put my head in my hands and wondered, *What I am I going to do now?*

Then suddenly, out of nowhere, I heard the thick German accent of my college electronics professor, Dr. Brown.

"Allan, someday you will regret not applying a greater effort in my classes. Your grades should be much better that this exam shows." My response to him haunted me.

"Professor, with all due respect, I do not like electronics or anything electrical."

Sitting on the crate, I could feel my head spinning. I was frozen in terror. No options. No idea what to do next.

I don't know how, but I quietly prayed to God for help and mercy. No sooner did I say my "Amen" than a thought popped into my head. I suddenly remembered what my high school math teacher, Mr. Hubiak, had always preached.

"When you are faced with a problem that overwhelms you, start with basic principles."

So, I stood up, the panel drawing in hand, and grabbed a roll of masking tape. I opened the drawing and taped it on the open door of the panel. I systematically went through the drawing, identifying each component, verifying that each was in the right location. Almost immediately I discovered something. There was a pattern of identical components on the drawing.

The left-hand row of each bank had the letter A after the relay's part number and the right-hand row had the letter B after the part number. When I looked at the panel, I found that all ninety-six relays had the A designation and not one relay had the B designation.

It became clear that one (and hopefully the only) problem was the lack of B relays.

I returned to the trailer office and phoned the manufacturer noted on the drawing. I explained the need to get a source for the relay. I gave them the part number and asked for a local distributor. They gave me a distributor's phone number and address that was a few miles away.

I called the distributor and gave him the part number, asking, "Do you have any of these relays in stock?"

"Yes, we do, but we do not have any of the A versions in stock, only Bs."

"Well, I have what might sound like a strange request. I have forty-eight of the A versions I want to swap for forty-eight of the B versions."

What he said next surprised me. His voice was indignant.

"Who are you, really? Is this a joke?"

"No, this is no joke, I am serious. What makes you think it's a joke?"

"I have a client who's been waiting for weeks to get a few dozen of the A version of this very relay. Your proposal seems incredible. It's just what I need! I seriously can't believe it!"

"Well, it's all true. Can I bring the forty-eight A relays for the swap?"

"How soon can you get here?"

When I arrived at the distributor and delivered the A relays, the man's face was awash in relief. It was no joke; I was the real thing. He immediately called his customer to tell him the good news, then retrieved my forty-eight B relays and thanked me profusely.

I returned to the plant and went directly to the burner deck. I inserted the *B* relays into their proper sockets. I took a nervous breath, then stood back, reached out, and pushed the large green start button to turn the system on. The whole panel lit up like a Christmas tree.

With a sigh of great relief, I silently offered up my prayer of praise and thanksgiving and headed to the trailer. I skipped across the muddy expanse between the plant and the trailer with the drawing rolled up under my arm and a smile on my face.

"Pete, the automatic burner ignition system is up and running. Passed all the diagnostic tests. We're ready to roll."

Pete's grin burst from his face and he offered a hearty pat on my back.

"Great job, Allan. That could have been a really sticky problem."

Although I didn't know it at the time, the senior vice president was watching me from the sidelines. Apparently, Pete had been asked to keep him informed of my performance.

As I reflect on this experience, I realized that when I asked God for help, I didn't receive exactly what I wanted, but I got something. That "something" was a clue that led me to a solution to the original problem I faced. God uses the resources we accumulate from our experiences and resurrects them from our personal "well" to reveal solutions at the precise moment we need them.

QUESTIONS to inspire:

Am I willing to trust someone when I am facing a dilemma?

Do I summon courage to act when I lack any understanding?

Am I willing to ask for help?

Do I see a divine or greater power at work for me?

Do I find inspiration for the future when I see evidence that the guidance I just experienced was precisely what was needed?

An Unexpected Ministry

When we had just moved to San Diego, we were thrilled to have found a loving church family. One Wednesday evening, we sat quietly in the back of the church, thanking God for leading us to our new spiritual home.

The minister offered a wonderful sermon. When he was done, he spoke the words that shattered my calm and pierced my soul.

"Choir, please offer up a hymn, and then Brother Allan Musterer will serve us."

I didn't see that coming!

In our church back home, we had a tradition similar to this one: on midweek services, a non-ordained brother would be called on to speak to the congregation. It was usually spontaneous. For twenty-seven years, it had been my greatest fear, to speak in front of a large group. For twenty-seven years, I had avoided a moment like this one.

As the choir began to sing, I somehow found the courage to make my way to the altar. I looked over at the forty parishioners seated before me.

The choir sang only one verse and then there was silence. My legs trembled beneath me and my mind went blank. *What am I going to say?* I wondered.

I opened my mouth and to my utter surprise, the words just flowed out of me. I was so wrapped in fear I didn't know what I had said.

But looking into the eyes of the attentive congregation, what I was saying was reaching them.

After about five minutes of speaking, I said the word, "AMEN!" and took my seat. When the service was over, I was humbled and overwhelmed with the kind words the parishioners offered me. Carol lovingly took my arm and whispered, "I am proud of you."

On the way home that evening, many experiences from the past surfaced in my soul.

I thought back to our marriage vows as we stood, bride and groom, in front of the minister. In his wedding address, the minister urged us to remember our pioneering heritage. Our parents and grandparents had been pioneers in establishing growth in our church in New Jersey. I myself never expected to become a minister due to my dreaded fear of public speaking.

Now that fear had been tested and I wondered what the future would hold. *Was this an omen for my future or just a one-time test?*

I also thought back to a time when Carol and I lived in a small apartment in Parsippany, New Jersey. My nights were spent attending classes toward a master's degree. Life was hectic. One free evening after a particularly difficult day at work, I was in a bad mood and was not very pleasant to Carol.

Carol's father was a minister in our church. Leaning on her experiences in her family, she had urged me, "Go visiting!"

I said, "Do you really think that's a good idea, considering my attitude right now?"

She said, "Yes! Do me a favor, do yourself a favor, and do God a favor, and go on a pastoral visit tonight!"

I didn't agree with Carol, but I acquiesced. I called my friend Rennie, a deacon in our church, and took him up on a previous invitation to join him on one of his pastoral visits. He was thrilled. We arranged for me to meet at his house.

When I arrived, Rennie told me he had previously arranged a visit to Doris, one of my childhood Sunday-school teachers. Some years before, Doris had married Joe, who was not interested in attending church, and she hoped a visit might help. I wondered what the visit would be like. I felt grateful that Rennie would be doing all the talking. I planned to just listen and silently pray.

When we arrived at Doris's house, Rennie and I prayed. He asked for the Holy Spirit to guide our words to inspire the man of the house to consider coming to church at least once. He prayed we would be used as a blessing for the family.

Doris welcomed us in, and we were introduced to Joe. We all sat down and then Doris quickly left the room, explaining she had to take care of the children.

As Rennie spoke with Joe, he was immediately confronted with adamant resistance. Joe was heated, mentioning his extensive readings of various religions and pointing to the many books in his bookcase. I felt so sorry for Rennie and quietly prayed for God's assistance. Each point Rennie attempted to make was met with anger and frustration. Rennie tried his best to keep the conversation void of controversy, but his every attempt failed. After about thirty minutes, Joe offered each of us a glass of water and left the room.

During Joe's brief absence, Rennie looked at me and said, "I am obviously not getting anywhere, so when Joe returns, you speak to him."

I was at a total loss, my greatest fear realized.

Joe returned with a glass of water for each of us.

I began, "Joe, I understand what you are saying. I can attest to your assessments of all these religious books you have read. I had a similar experience when I went to college. I attended a university in Pennsylvania. Not one of our churches was within my reach. I decided to attend each of the seven churches in town on successive Sunday mornings. I entered each with an open mind and heart and a hungry soul."

As I spoke, Joe, leaning forward in his chair, was paying intense attention to my narrative.

I continued, "I found that each church offered me something of value, something that satisfied a longing in me. One, for instance, had a spectacular choir. The music soothed my soul, but the sermon was uninspiring, simply reporting on the news of the week. Another church had an extraordinary speaker who delivered an entertaining sermon, but it was lacking in spiritual content. I discovered that each church I visited satisfied some aspect of my being, but all failed to fully satisfy my spiritual hunger. It showed me that what I had been experiencing in our church had been satisfying my whole need."

Joe was now nodding his head in agreement with my message.

I mentioned that I didn't feel that type of satisfaction until I began to read transcripts of sermons from our church.

"Joe, I feel that with your deep interest, curiosity, and searching soul, you owe it to yourself and your family to explore what our church has to offer. Why don't you and your family come at least once to see what I have found to be so valuable?"

Joe responded with a willingness, but made it clear he would make no promises. Joe asked Doris and the children to join us and the deacon offered up a prayer. We shook hands and departed.

On my drive home, I reflected on the evening. I felt that God used my experience to touch Joe's heart. I realized that when I was willing, God could make use of me and my experiences.

Carol was right; by placing me into God's hands to do His work, He transformed my heart and attitude. I returned home with a renewed outlook and spirit.

Joe and the family attended at least one of our services, but he apparently did not find what he was looking for. Though somewhat disappointed, I somehow knew that I had been transformed by the experience.

As we made our home in San Diego, I would be called to speak in our new church a few more times. Then surprisingly, within a few months, Carol and I were asked if we would be willing to start a new congregation in a different neighborhood. It was at that moment that the words from our minister's wedding address surfaced in my mind: "Remember your pioneer heritage."

The following month, I was ordained into the deacon ministry, and the following year I was ordained a priest.

Over the ensuing years, Carol and I started three new congregations in San Diego. God blessed us as we worked together and experienced many extraordinary moments doing the Lord's work. Carol truly was the perfect gift with her talents for supporting the ministry. Now after fifty years together, we still marvel at how God engineered our finding each other and the life we have enjoyed.

Upon reflection, the Bible passage in Isaiah 55:8–9 shows the wisdom of bringing God into our plans and not relying on our own imperfect ones.

> [8] "For My thoughts *are* not your thoughts, nor *are* your ways My ways," says the LORD.
> [9] "For *as* the heavens are higher than the earth, so are My ways higher than your ways, and My thoughts than your thoughts."
>
> Isaiah 55:8–9 (NKJV)

QUESTIONS to inspire:

Can I trust God when I am thrust into a situation for which I am unprepared to act?

Do I have the trust to decide when I lack direction and understanding?

Am I willing to see God at work within me and for me?

Can I enjoy the unfolding guidance when I experience it?

If you're going through hell, keep going.

~Anonymous

If you want to achieve something, you're going to run into roadblocks, but you have to learn to pivot and explore your option.

~ Hannah Bronfman

Our greatest glory is not in never falling, but in rising every time we fall.

~Oliver Goldsmith

Chapter 5

Education Paths

The education path you follow is intended to guide you to your career and professional goals. How do you choose that path? Often, we have a preconceived idea, but even if well thought out, it may be lacking in content and scope. Trusting God and His guidance makes for an efficient path to our education goal. That guidance may lead you to people whose experience can shed new light on your plans. It also aids in developing the patience needed when unexpected challenges arise and decisions must be made. Do I stick to the plan or do I make a change?

College Surprises

When I arrived at Bucknell University and met my schoolmates, I discovered almost all had attended very high-end prep schools. I was intimidated, to say the least. Even before my first class began, I felt my high school education was lacking.

The first class was calculus, taught by Dr. Gold, head of the mathematics department. Calculus classes were composed of engineering students and math majors. So, every class posed the highest level of competition.

Initially, I thought I was doing very well. All the homework was easy. And then came the first exam. I moved through it swiftly and was convinced I got it all right. A few days later, I was surprised to find that I got most of the simple problems wrong but all the difficult ones right. This was very puzzling. I continued to study more intently. Then the second test came. Same result. Most easy problems were wrong.

This time Dr. Gold summoned me to his office. "Allan, did you have a course in calculus in high school?

"Yes, I did."

Dr. Gold looked perplexed.

I confessed, "Dr. Gold, I just don't understand how I am failing to do the easy problems correctly."

"I suggest you take more time doing the easier problems. Recheck them a second time before you move on to tackle the challenging ones."

I took the professor's advice and my grades immediately improved.

This experience helped me quell the feeling that my education had been inferior to my classmates'. I found new confidence going into my second semester—only to find that confidence challenged once more.

Next subject: Applied Engineering Mechanics – Statics.

The course required the application of calculus and a functional understanding of geometry and trigonometry. It was taught by Mr. Frank Ahimaz, a professor from India. He was an excellent teacher with a swift teaching style and a thick accent that was just plain hard to understand. Even so, I felt that I grasped the material. I found the homework relatively easy. I acquired a reputation among my fellow students as a resource when they ran into trouble.

I enjoyed the class because I was learning interesting concepts. The application of engineering principles to structures such as bridges, towers, and beams was fascinating. However, that enjoyment was short-lived. The first exam proved to be a disaster. When grades were passed out, I was shocked to see a large D on the cover of my exam book.

What in heaven's name happened? How can this be? There must be some mistake.

After class, I went to see Mr. Ahimaz in his office, stating, "I am very surprised at the grade on my test."

Sympathetically, he said, "Sure, I understand. But don't expect me to change the grade. It is up to you to work harder to get the grade up."

To my utter dismay, each successive test resulted in low grades, despite my efforts. I continued to have a very clear understanding of the material, but when I entered each exam, I somehow failed to apply what I understood.

At the end of the semester, I got a D on the final exam and that became the grade on my transcript. I feared my engineering career was in jeopardy. I failed to understand what was happening. Why did I understand the material, yet almost fail each exam?

At that time, I didn't apply Solomon's Recipe, most likely because it was not yet clear to me how it worked or even that it existed.

Next Class: Applied Engineering Mechanics – Dynamics and Gas Dynamics

The dynamics course at Bucknell was taught by Mr. Edward Staiano. He was a very difficult but excellent teacher (although I didn't exactly realize the *excellent* part while I was in his class).

Mr. Staiano had a reputation for being inflexible and hard on students. Consequently, he earned the sarcastic nickname "Easy Ed Staiano."

I once again had success learning the concepts. I thoroughly understood the lectures and was able to do the homework with ease. I continued to help my classmates with the homework.

Not surprisingly this time, the first exam was a disaster, yet it still stung. Mr. Staiano passed out our exam bluebooks with the grades in dark blue ink on the cover. I was shocked to see a large 0 on the cover and the words scrawled below it, "There is nothing correct in this book. See me at once."

I went to Mr. Staiano's office with trepidation. I entered his office and sat down sheepishly in front of his desk. I held a slight hope that he might be able to point me in the right direction. Maybe, just maybe, he might be able to help?

He asked, "Allan, what happened in the exam?"

"I don't know. I felt I understood the material and was able to do the homework, but I can't understand why I did so poorly on the exam."

I guess this was something he had heard from lazy students before, and he huffed, "Well Allan, if I am the one to keep you from becoming an engineer, so be it!"

I sat there in shock at his cold response. Any thought of him offering help evaporated. I saw my whole life crumbling before me. The shame of failure. The shock of defeat when I was so convinced I knew what I was doing.

I left his office deeply discouraged. I could see visions of our hometown newspaper with headlines: "Musterer Flunks Out of Bucknell." *How could I shame my parents, who sacrificed so much to give me this opportunity?* As I closed the door, a deep pain invaded my gut.

I left the building numb and started my walk home.

Then, from somewhere deep within me, a prayer rose up. *Dear God, I trusted You when I chose this school, and when I chose engineering for a career. I just don't understand this. And yet, I still believe You have a plan for me. I am sure this will somehow work out. I pray for Your guidance.*

By the time I made it back to my room, I felt a shift. I somehow had decided that this was not going to keep me from becoming an engineer. I was determined to see it through. I took Mr. Staiano's cold comment as a challenge and not as a death sentence. I was going to prove him wrong. Surely my trust in God would guide me forward.

Despite my efforts to conquer whatever was causing my test experiences, I failed the rest of the exams and received a final grade of F. My only recourse was to face taking the class over again. The cold reality was that Easy Ed was the only one who taught dynamics and the second chance was the only one.

The next semester, I sat in dynamics again and also took an elective. I chose a class in statistics. The course was given in the psychology department with Professor Wendall Smith.

With all my background in advanced mathematics, statistics should have been a breeze. As it turned out, the same thing happened in statistics as in dynamics when the time came for the first exam. I got a D. Again, failure reared its ugly head. *What in the world was going on?*

Professor Smith invited me to his office after class. When he expressed confusion about my performance on the test, he didn't shun me, discourage me, or disbelieve me. He was instead interested in helping me.

"Allan, walk me through how you take an exam. Not the preparation at home, but what you do when you walk into the exam room and how you approach the test material."

I explained, "I quickly look at the first problem and immediately work on solving it. Initially it seems quite simple, but inevitably I reach a point where there is something unexpected. I continue to labor until I fear I will not finish, then I go on to the next one."

"Ah! I see what's happening. Your emotions are getting the best of you. I have a strategy I suggest you try."

This was getting interesting, as I wondered, *Is this God's guidance, seeing that I met this professor and took this course?*

"When you take your next exam, regardless of the course, follow this procedure. Before you take your pencil or pen from your pocket, read the entire exam. Read each problem with the idea that you will be placing them in a hierarchy of easy to difficult. When you have done this, begin with the easiest one. The instant you encounter something unexpected, stop. Go on to the next problem in the hierarchy. Continue this till you finish. Then return to the unfinished problems, and I think you will see that you will be able to complete them successfully."

"Thank you, Mr. Smith. I'll try this in two days, when I have my next dynamics test."

During the next exam, I applied what I learned from Professor Smith. The first time around I didn't complete a single problem. The second time through, however, I finished all of them. I turned in my test with a renewed sense of hope.

At the next dynamics class, I received my test booklet with a 100 percent, grade A. I was ecstatic. Mr. Staiano had a word for me.

"I don't know what you did, Allan, but I am suspicious." He thought I had cheated.

On the next statistics exam I got an A and met again with Professor Smith. I asked him why he thought his method was working for me.

He explained, "Allan, you panicked when a problem was different from what you expected. That panic overwhelmed your ability to think. Doing it this way, you are managing your panic or your emotional response to test taking."

I continued to get an A on my dynamics tests and ended up with a C for a final grade.

My experiences with Easy Ed, however, were not over.

The following year, gas dynamics was on my schedule. And yes, it was only taught by none other than Easy Ed Staiano. I entered the course with renewed confidence.

Mr. Staiano told us in the beginning of the semester that he was giving only two exams: the midterm and the final. The midterm was to count in the final grade. His homework assignments during the semester were very challenging, but I found that I was able to grasp the lessons.

When we sat for the midterm exam, everyone was apprehensive. A lot was riding on the outcome. The exam had three problems. The first two were worth 25 percent each and the third was 50 percent. The first two were easy for me, but the third was a real challenge. It was composed of two long, complex energy equations shown as equal. The challenge was to work each side mathematically to prove that they were equal. After working on it for a good part of the allotted time, I concluded that they were not equal. Believing that Easy Ed would be willing to put a "ringer" like that on a test, I struck a line through the equal sign and wrote the words, "These equations are not equal." It was a gutsy call, but I felt I knew the mentality of Easy Ed better than my classmates.

When the exam grades were posted, I had a perfect score and all my classmates had a score of 50. All of them forced the two energy equations to be equal. They couldn't believe that Easy Ed would play a trick on them on such an important exam.

Mr. Staiano eventually told us that he had made an error in transcribing the equations and intended them to be equal. But since one student (me) got it right, he wasn't willing to discard it from the midterm grade. Hence, everyone had to accept an F on their midterm, except me.

My fellow students were not very happy, but graciously didn't fault me for getting it right.

Both courses, dynamics and gas dynamics, forced me to face failing ways of taking tests. I changed how I prepared for and faced exams. My new perspective's success was evidenced in the marked improvement in the grades I achieved in all successive courses.

I also learned that a student's grades did not always accurately reflect what they had learned. Sometimes other psychological factors were at play. This became an important lesson for me to pass on to others.

I never forgot that one singular moment when I could have given up my dream to become an engineer. I could have taken my teacher's words as definitive truth and quit his class or left school altogether. But on that walk home, God reached into my heart and whispered His guidance to stay the course. Despite all the evidence pointing toward possible failure, trusting my Lord allowed me to keep walking, to keep trying, to reach for success, having no idea how it might arrive. In a way, my entire future, my entire career rested on that moment when I heard God's whisper to have faith. And I did.

QUESTIONS to inspire:

Am I willing to trust when failing?

Am I willing to persevere even when I lack complete understanding?

Am I willing to ask for help?

Am I able to see a divine or greater power at work for me?

Am I inspired and encouraged by the guidance when I experience it?

Graduate School Disaster

Just when I thought I knew the best path for my future, disaster struck. When I became a member of the nuclear department at Foster Wheeler, I quickly realized that if I ever wanted a real promotion, I had better get a master's degree. So I set out to find a way to make that happen. It was important that I find a school nearby that had evening classes, so I could work by day. Foster Wheeler offered some assistance with tuition benefits, so going to graduate school in the evenings was a simple decision. I decided on Newark College of Engineering (NCE) in Newark, New Jersey.

I decided to take advanced heat transfer and a course in nuclear reactor theory. The advanced heat transfer course at NCE was immediately beneficial to my work and I received a reasonable grade. Nuclear reactor theory, however, was a very different situation.

Nuclear reactor theory required the application of very advanced mathematics and a clear understanding of nuclear radiation. I had solid backgrounds in both subjects from my undergraduate education.

Nuclear reactor theory was taught by a brilliant Chinese professor, Dr. Hu. The complexity of the subject matter required a good connection between teacher and student. Unfortunately for me, Dr. Hu's heavy accent created a severe lack of understanding. The tests and the homework seriously challenged my ability to comprehend the subject matter. Week after week I struggled, reaching out to my classmates, but even that didn't really help.

Frustrated and fearful, I entered the final exams with trepidation. When the final grades were posted, I somehow achieved a grade of D. Even though I didn't fail, the low grade sealed the end of my pursuit of an engineering graduate degree.

I was shattered. *What now?*

Very discouraged at this turn of events, I prayed for a new direction. I had to come up with a new plan, and fast. But, what to do? Then I remembered someone once telling me, "If you want an advanced degree, get it as soon as possible after graduation; otherwise, life happens and you'll never find the time again."

This thought triggered my decision to pursue a master's in business administration. I investigated available programs and applied to the evening MBA program at Fairleigh Dickenson University (FDU), specializing in business management.

I began my master's program at FDU in the fall of 1967. I took my knowledge of how I read into account. I was always a slow reader because I focused on comprehension over speed. This had served me well in my study of the sciences. I therefore decided to enroll in two courses per semester. One required little reading, the other a lot. This provided a balance.

My plan was to get to the office early each morning, so I had an hour or more to study and do my homework and be prepared for each evening's class. I left work at four thirty and drove to the campus where I could study a bit more before my two classes.

I reached home after class around ten thirty or eleven at night. I was fortunate to get along without much sleep. Fridays and weekends, I snuck in any work that I couldn't squeeze in during the week. It was a very busy time in my life.

I found the subject matter in the MBA curriculum quite easy compared to the intense engineering classes. I also seemed to have an edge over my classmates, most of whom were business majors in undergraduate school. I had the benefit of an education that taught the scientific method of study, and engineering provided process thinking. With the wisdom I had gained at Bucknell in the process of learning, I achieved excellent grades despite the long hours and hectic schedule.

By the end of my years at FDU, I graduated cum laude, in May of 1970. Within a few weeks after graduation, I was promoted and sent to San Diego, California.

My trust in God helped me to recover from the disappointment of losing out on an engineering graduate degree. His guidance moved me quickly into the MBA program that positioned me for the promotion that brought me to San Diego and a whole new life.

What first appeared to be a negative disaster ultimately revealed itself as a big positive. I took this lesson with me. I learned that even when life seems to be pushing you off your chosen tracks, you can find new ones, possibly even better ones, if you have faith.

QUESTIONS to inspire:

Am I willing to trust that my Plan *A* was not best for me?

Am I willing to accept, in the face of not understanding, that Plan *B* will be best?

Am I able to see a divine or greater power at work for me?

Can I enjoy the unfolding guidance when I experience it and put my best effort to make the new plan work?

God wants to speak to you, but you must listen. Not with your ears but, with your heart.

Chapter 6

Finding Your Way in Business

Your place in the business world has a powerful impact on the rest of your life. It is the means for your financial sustenance and hopefully your personal satisfaction. It is therefore critical that you utilize every asset available to you to ensure your success and the value you bring to your work. Trusting in God in this area may seem strange at first, but His guidance is not limited. I have found that His guidance is essential even in the business world.

Changing Career Plans

When I was fourteen, I thought I would become a pharmacist. Seriously and completely. I was convinced I would become a pharmacist. I didn't even really know what a pharmacist did; it just seemed like an impressive career. Entering a pharmacy as a young boy was a treat for me. Everything was so clean, efficient, and organized.

The pharmacist was always impressively dressed in a white shirt and tie and wore a distinctive white lab coat. Important things must be happening, I surmised.

I imagined myself in that coat. It felt admirable. Dignified, even.

I had no real idea what it would take to become a pharmacist, and yet anytime someone would ask me, "What do you want to be when you grow up?" I proudly answered, "I want to be a pharmacist!'"

Then an unexpected bit of inspiration appeared in the form of my cousin, Don. He was five years older and was attending Newark College of Engineering. Don's mother, my Aunt Helen, was a widow who suffered from debilitating arthritis in her hips. Aunt Helen had great difficulty walking, requiring two canes just to navigate her small apartment. Following her husband's untimely death, she was faced with raising Don and his younger brother, Fred, all by herself. She faced real struggle both physically and economically. Fortunately, the owner of their apartment building had compassion and employed Aunt Helen as the apartment superintendent. With her mobility so severely compromised, Don and his brother Fred performed all the physical activities needed of the superintendent.

Aunt Helen couldn't drive either, so she relied on her sons to get her around. From time to time Don or Fred would bring their mother to our house so the two sisters could visit. One thing was clear: they didn't have money for college.

We were all delighted when Don received a scholarship from General Electric. The terms of his scholarship required him to work at their small-appliance design facility as an intern while attending school. This gave him hands-on experience in the real world of engineering. I so admired Don. Facing overwhelming adversity, he had found a way to excel. And he was becoming an engineer. I was curious.

One day, Don brought his mother over for a visit. While the sisters sat together chatting on our back porch, Don and I went upstairs to my room to talk. In the cozy nook of my bedroom library, Don told me about his work at GE and all about his engineering classes. As he explained in detail how he designed intricate components of toasters and miniature ovens and other small appliances, my eyes got wider. He described how the classes he was taking equipped him with the ability to design solutions to the issues he faced on the job. I sat there, listening in utter fascination. Maybe God was starting to whisper in my ear. Maybe I didn't want to become a pharmacist after all. The more Don shared his experiences, the more I wanted to become an engineer. By the end of the afternoon with my cousin, my whole career focus had changed.

The next morning, I eagerly shared with my parents my desire to become an engineer. I wasn't met with the wild enthusiasm I had been expecting. Instead, I think my father was testing my desire or dedication to go to college.

As we sat across from one another at the kitchen table, my father said, "Okay, we will send you to college, but if you don't go to college, we will buy you a new car when you graduate high school."

It didn't take much thought for me to turn down the offer of a new car. My mind was made up. It was the beginning of an awakening of trust. Trust between me and God. I felt a pull to change directions and trusted that even though I had no idea how, with the Lord beside me, I would make it happen.

QUESTIONS to inspire:

Am I willing to trust God when faced with a big change in my plans?

Am I willing to act when I lack complete understanding?

Do I to see a divine or greater power at work for me?

Can I enjoy the unfolding guidance when I experience it?

Choosing an Employer

My senior year at college brought a new challenge. The time had come to start thinking about choosing an employer. Companies sent recruiters to Bucknell, looking for qualified employees. Each competed for the best of the new crop of graduates. I tried not to worry—only my whole future was at stake.

What made the process even more terrifying was my grade point average. Every employer would request a copy of the transcript of my grades. My troubles with my test-taking skills early on in college left me with an unimpressive, low GPA. In fact, when I compared myself to my fellow graduates, I found myself just below the average. What kind of prospects would this leave me?

As the recruiters made their pitches, I discovered that there were many diverse jobs for mechanical engineers. Ultimately, I was drawn to seven companies in as many industries: power, computers, aerospace, chemicals, building products, heavy construction, military equipment, and steel. My preliminary interviews were successful, and I was invited for follow-up interviews. I embarked on seven trips around the country for in-plant interviews.

First, I visited a large computer company in New York State. Three managers challenged me, asking how I would solve a problem they were experiencing in their department. Their interest in me was piqued when I offered my solutions. They wanted me to come back again, but they had not yet received my GPA transcript.

Next, I visited a company in the building-products industry in Maine. They made plastic skylights. I left with the feeling that this was a distinct possibility for a career. My next trip was to a steel company in Pennsylvania. It was an amazing experience, seeing the intricacies of a steel plant and learning about the varied possibilities they offered for mechanical engineers.

Then I visited a company in the power industry in New Jersey, not far from my parents' home. The company designed and built power plants, chemical process plants, and refineries. The division I interviewed with was the power-plant group. They offered a wide range of opportunities, but the one thing that caught my interest was their training program. It was a nine-month program that gave an engineer a taste of various aspects of the company, from design to field service and manufacturing. This appealed to me because it didn't require me to be productive instantly. My low grades had given me a feeling that my education and my ability to function as an engineer may be less than what I imagined. This interview was very positive, and I hoped for an offer.

I visited a second company in New Jersey, in heavy construction. Although I was impressed with the personnel, I was taken aback by the facilities. The offices were cramped, barely enough for two chairs, a desk, and a file cabinet. I left with mixed emotions and little in the way of expectations.

I traveled to upstate New York to visit a company that supplied specialized equipment to the military. The equipment was fascinating in its complexity. However, the offices were housed in a crumbling building. The wooden floors were severely worn, and steam pipes with the insulation crumbling off ran across one interviewer's desk. Again, I left this company with conflicting emotions.

I next went to Cleveland, Ohio, to visit a company in the chemical industry. The company made plastic containers. The plant tour was interesting, but I was not impressed with what I saw of Cleveland. Again, mixed feelings accompanied me on the way back to school.

My final visit was to Bethpage, Long Island. This was an aerospace company that was building aircraft and space vehicles. My visit was extraordinary. The plant was immaculate. The project I was interviewed for was the design and construction of the lunar excursion module. That was the vehicle known as the LEM that later landed on the moon. The prospect of working on such a potentially historic project was exhilarating.

After each interview, I sent transcripts of my grades and letters of appreciation. Then the waiting game commenced.

After a few months, offers of employment began to arrive. To my great shock, six out of the seven companies I interviewed for offered me employment. I was overjoyed.

I knew it was time to return to prayer.

I looked at my list of options and zeroed in on two. The highest offer came from the aerospace company. The lowest was from the power company. I compared my offers with my fellow students. I had garnered both the highest and the lowest offers in my class. I put all my trust in the Lord and asked for guidance to accept the offer that would be best for my future. Then I waited.

Thoughts swirled around me. It was a lot to weigh, and I didn't know how to make the decision. The power company offer gave me the opportunity to spend nine months in a training program. That gave me time to prove myself. It would be an easy commute from my parents' home. Paying them rent would help pay back some of money they spent on my college education. But a big downside was the financial offer.

The aerospace offer was exciting. No doubt, it would be a highly prestigious job. Not to mention the fact that, by far, they offered the highest salary. On the downside, it was on Long Island, which would require a long commute or an expensive apartment.

After prayerful deliberation and listening to the Lord, I decided on the lowest offer—the power company. I know to some it seemed odd to choose the job that offered the least prestigious projects and the least amount of money. But I loved the idea of paying my parents back and the whisper in my ear from the Lord was something I could not turn away from.

I spent ten years at this company. And it changed me in every important way. Though I didn't know it at the time, within a year of graduation, my salary would eclipse that of my fellow students. The company sent me to my dream home, San Diego, where I live to this day. By getting quiet, by praying and listening, I was able to hear one of the most important whispers of my life.

QUESTIONS to inspire:

When facing a big decision, am I willing to get quiet and listen to the whispers of the Lord's Spirit?

Am I willing to act, going into something lacking complete understanding of where it will lead?

Am I able to accept a divine and greater power at work for me?

Can I enjoy the unfolding guidance when I experience it?

Beginning a Career

So, it became attractive to me when Foster Wheeler Corporation offered me employment that started with a nine-month training program. This seemed wise because it gave me the opportunity to get my feet wet before there were great expectations.

Since the company headquarters were in New Jersey, I could live at my parents' home and pay them back for their investment in my education.

I reported to work at Foster Wheeler the third week of June 1965. My first week on the job was orientation of the company structure and the various departments and their function. On Friday that week, I joined the three other trainees as we were led to the service department.

We sat in the manager's office at a large table.

The manager spoke matter-of-factly, without emotion. "I need all of you immediately in the field."

He looked at me and Lenny who sat beside me, reached across his desk, and handed each of a us a sealed white envelope.

"You two are going to Pasadena, California, and you are flying out Sunday."

At first this was quite exciting, as I had always dreamed of visiting California. Then I realized that I would have to leave my new Pontiac Bonneville convertible in New Jersey!

When I drove to my parents' home that night, a mix of emotions swelled up in my head. So much had just happened in the brief span of an hour. I was excited to be going to Pasadena. But the nagging concern was this would be my first big test. What did the future hold? Would I be ready without the additional training I was counting on?

Sunday morning, July 4, 1965, my parents drove me to Newark airport, where Lenny and I boarded a plane to Los Angeles. When we exited the plane, I was shocked to see a man who was the spitting image of my father, but a bit older. It was my Uncle Walter, and my cousin Fred was standing next to him. Unknown to me, my dad had called his brother and told him of my assignment. Lenny and I spent that day and the Monday holiday with the family.

Tuesday morning, Lenny and I left our hotel and walked the four blocks south on Arroyo Seco Parkway to the Pasadena Municipal Power Plant situated at the north end of the Pasadena Freeway. Foster Wheeler had built the steam generator and cooling towers for the new gas-fired power plant on the site.

We found the Foster Wheeler trailer field office and met Arno, the senior service engineer managing the project. Arno welcomed us and introduced us to another service engineer, Hank, prior to taking us on a plant tour.

The first shock was when we were told that we were going to be in Pasadena for six months. We had expected to be there for just a few weeks. That meant we needed to rent an apartment and get transportation. Lenny and I pooled our money and bought a used car and rented an apartment just behind the plant in South Pasadena.

The first challenge on the job for me was to overcome my fear of heights. There were no stairs on this boiler structure to get from one floor to the next. The only way around was via a manlift. Manlifts are simply a vertical conveyor belt running from the ground floor to the top floor through small platforms on each floor. The belt had a succession of hand grips and small boxes. When you needed to go up, you stood on the platform and watched for the hand grip to arrive. The belt moved continuously. When the hand grip came up you would grab it and then step onto the box that followed about four feet below the grip. Then when you reached the floor you wanted to exit, you just reversed the procedure.

When I mastered the manlift, the work began. Arno assigned Lenny and me small work assignments with both him and Hank. We did numerous tasks related to the boiler performance and preparations to solve a vibration problem that had developed in the boiler. We did projects that included installation of temperature measuring grids and their associated cabling, vibration measurements, and inspections of the internals of the boiler.

After we concluded our vibration measurements, I was tasked with writing a report and submitting the vibration results to the home office. The engineers at the home office used my report as a basis to design a baffle to dissipate the vibrations that we had measured.

A week passed and the baffle drawings arrived at the office. Arno assigned me the task of installing the baffle in the boiler. I had three days to make the preparations prior to the arrival of the baffle plates from the manufacturing plant in New Jersey.

First, I examined the drawings. The baffle was made up of a series of steel plates. The drawings showed their location inside the boiler. I surveyed the interior of the boiler to identify the exact location for the baffle plates. The challenge I faced was the precise maneuvering necessary to get the longest plate into position. Once that was in place, installing the rest of the assembly would be a rather simple task.

I considered the challenge facing me and wondered how I would achieve success. I again relied on my trust in God. As I consulted Him, I realized that if I could make a replica of the largest plate, I could test the maneuvering inside the boiler and master the exact movements before the actual plates arrived.

Coincidentally, there was an incinerator on site. I thought there might be an opportunity to find material for the replica I needed. I walked hopefully over to the incinerator and promptly noticed a long piece of heavy, stiff cardboard lying off to the side. I took it back to the trailer and measured out the largest baffle plate dimensions onto the cardboard. It was the perfect size; it just needed some trimming. I requisitioned a power saw from the plant and proceeded to cut my replica plate to size.

I took the cardboard replica into the boiler and maneuvered it dozens of ways before I finally got it to work. Once the longest plate was inside and in position, the installation of the other plates, being shorter, would be a simple matter.

Using my experience with the replica, I generated a work plan and developed staffing requirements and hours to produce a realistic budget. After adding a liberal contingency, I presented my plan and budget to Arno.

Unbeknownst to me, Arno added more contingency to the budget prior to forwarding it to his boss.

A week later, the plates arrived. I inspected them against the drawings and verified that they were acceptable for the installation. I assembled a crew of laborers and began the installation. The preliminary planning made an early completion of the installation possible. It came in well under my original budget, without the need for my contingency. The bottom line as seen by the home office was even more impressive due to Arno's added contingency.

Arno took no credit for my performance and gave me all the benefit of the project's success. Although I didn't know it at the time, this caused the senior vice president to take an interest in me and my work, and he watched my every move that followed.

Arno and I took another round of vibration measurements at specific locations following the startup of the boiler. The results revealed the success of the design and installation of the baffle as a solution for the vibration issue.

QUESTIONS to inspire:

Am I willing to trust, even when the path ahead is unsure?

Can I choose to decide when I just can't understand?

As divine guidance presents itself, can I follow and act upon it?

A Defiant Client

In the business world, eventually you find yourself in a position where you must stand up for what is right, even when those around you insist on doing what's wrong.

In the winter of 1965–66, I was assigned to support the final stages of the installation of a coal-fired power plant on the banks of the Hudson River. I worked under the guidance of a great man that I deeply respected, Pete Peterson. On a raw and blustery winter Monday morning, our team of engineers arrived at the field office. As we took our first sips of coffee and waited for Pete, our fearless leader, to arrive, the office door opened and in walked Bill, the senior vice president.

We were taken off guard. While Bill was usually a very personable man with a smile that put you at ease, today he wore only a grimace. His eyes were cast downward.

What's going on? we all thought.

Bill sat down and guided us all to do the same.

"Over the weekend, Pete lost both his wife and his father. It was all very unexpected, and he is well, but he won't be coming in."

"Of course, he needs time," one of the engineers chimed in.

Bill continued, "No, what I mean to say is that he won't be coming back to the job."

He sighed. "He actually requested to return to his old assignment in Japan."

We sat in shock. No one was sure what to say or how to process what we had just heard. What would we do without our leader? As the youngest on the team, I definitely felt dependent on his guidance.

Bill asked each of us what we were working on, and then he asked me to show him around the plant. We left the trailer office and headed out.

Once we were out of sight of the others, Bill stopped and turned to me. "Allan, I don't need a tour; I designed this boiler. I wanted to get you alone because I want you to manage this project."

To say that I was in shock was an understatement. And I was more than just a little confused when I replied, "I appreciate that, but do you know that I am still in my training program and all of the others have seniority on me?"

The truth was that inside I wasn't sure I could handle the job. I was still fairly new. Did I have what it took? I knew it could be a rough job and I wondered if I would be able to handle everything a manager had to handle.

Bill was matter-of-fact about it. "You may be on our training program, but when you woke up this morning, you were a senior service engineer. And you have a retroactive pay raise accordingly. I want you to manage this project because I trust you."

I saw by the look in his eye that he needed me to step up.

"Of course, Mr. Stevens, I promise to do my best. And thank you for this opportunity."

As he walked away, he tossed off, "If any of the team members give you a hard time, let me know."

As I walked back to the trailer, I prayed for the extra courage I knew I would need to suddenly take on a leadership role, especially when I had the least seniority. As I prayed, I felt a wave of support surround me. I remembered how the Lord had guided me to success with a previous challenge on this very job.

Over the next weeks, I enjoyed the full support of the team, save for one very angry, very resistant man. I did my best to win him over, but he dug his heels in and attempted to sabotage my work. I was nervous about taking the steps necessary to get him reassigned. Then I became quiet and felt the Lord beside me. Calmly, without incident, I took those steps, and he was reassigned.

With the remaining team members all on board, we were able to complete the project successfully and the other team members moved on to other projects. I felt a sense of pride. I had handled a team. I knew I was being guided and was grateful. I remained alone to finish up some final project details, thinking that this project was about to wrap up.

What I didn't know was that big trouble was lurking around the corner.

Sam, the on-site manager for Orange & Rockland Utilities, had unfortunately made some operational decisions that were inconsistent with our best practices. The result was one of the eight coal burners was damaged and had to be taken out of service. Despite having one less burner, they continued to operate the plant at over 100 percent capacity. This put the integrity of the boiler at risk.

I felt my voice shaking, but I got on the phone with Sam to warn him. "Listen, it's really important that you decrease plant operation, and I mean no more than 90 percent capacity, preferably less, or we may see some heavy consequences."

Sam was short with me. "No, we won't be doing that, thank you." And he hung up.

I knew he was counting on his pushy demeanor to win the day—and the fact that he thought I might just slink away, a young manager without the courage to push back.

I took a moment. I wondered, *Maybe I should just let it go and not have a confrontation. Maybe I didn't need the aggravation, and all would be okay. No, I have to take a stand.*

Yet I felt a knot grow in the pit of my stomach. I knew that if Sam continued to act this way, we could be in serious trouble. I wasn't sure what to do. Somehow, I knew it was an important moment, and that I needed to find the courage to face Sam. And I needed to document this.

I decided to type up a letter to Sam as the representative of the utility. I explained in detail what was happening inside the boiler, operating at the elevated capacity with only seven burners. I warned that after several more hours of operation at current levels, the accumulated slag (waste) would bridge across the boiler's base, automatically shutting down the boiler. The resulting repairs would take six to eight weeks of round-the-clock effort, and the boiler and plant would be idled for that duration. I told him that continued operation above the recommended 90-percent level beyond the next twenty-four hours would absolve our company of any responsibility for the consequences.

I made copies for the managers at our home office, including Bill, and a copy for my personal file. With the original and copies in hand, I marched to Sam's office and presented them to him. I asked him to sign them as his acknowledgment that he received them.

Sam willingly signed the letter and copies and waved me off. I left him with the original and filed a copy in my cabinet. The rest of the copies I mailed to our office.

That detail done, I waited, staying on the jobsite round-the-clock. I felt that I needed to be there the moment my predictions came to fruition. In anticipation, I packed a suitcase and a cot that would allow me to stay overnight in our trailer office for a few days.

As I had feared, Sam and his staff decided to ignore my letter and continued to operate the boiler at the elevated rate. Within a week and half, my prediction became a reality.

The boiler shut down and the power plant could operate only their two old boilers. It was a mess. A big old mess that required six weeks of round-the-clock work to bring the boiler back online. Eventually the slag was removed, a new burner was installed to replace the damaged one, and the whole system was retested prior to release back to the utility.

Some six months later, I was working as an engineer in the nuclear department. One day, one of our company's corporate attorneys appeared in my office. He asked me if I still had a copy of that signed letter that I had delivered to the manager at Orange & Rockland Utilities six months ago.

"Yes, I do." I opened my file drawer and pulled out a folder and found the copy. "Do you mean this one?"

He took a good look at the letter, and as he perused it, a big smile erupted on his face.

"Yes, that's it. You might not believe this, but you just saved the company from a multi-million-dollar lawsuit. Thank you!"

He left quickly to bring the good news to the upper management. I breathed a sigh of relief, grateful that I kept a copy. With a bit of pride, I prayed a brief prayer of thanksgiving that I had followed the impulses from my God to react as I did when challenged.

Reflecting on this experience, the promotion to manage the project under very stressful conditions gave me confidence in my abilities. I felt God had placed me in these situations to help me grow. I acknowledge God's hand in this intricate series of events that helped me to locate courage when I feared I might not have enough.

QUESTIONS to inspire:

Can I trust God's guidance in the heat of adversity and when I am unsure?

Am I willing to decide and act boldly even without clear understanding?

Does a divine or greater power at work for me encourage me to be assertive?

When the guidance received leads to success, do I find further inspiration for the future?

What Do You Want to Do in This Company?

I was approaching the end of my nine-month training program at Foster Wheeler, working on some mundane tasks in the service department and filing final reports, when suddenly Bill Stevens, the senior vice president, walked into my office. "Allan, come with me."

I followed Bill into the main corridor. I felt a mix of fear and concern. I had no idea what he wanted. *Had I somehow made some serious mistake?*

Bill turned to me. "Allan, you are too valuable to this company to be working where you are now. What do you want to do in this company?"

Partially in shock, I stood there for what seemed to me to be minutes, not knowing what to say. Then, without really thinking, I blurted out, "I'm not sure, but if I were your son, where would you want me to be?"

He thought for a moment, then he began walking and waved me to follow along. "Come with me. The nuclear department is the future of this company."

We walked down the corridor and into the nuclear department manager's office. His name was Jack.

Bill announced, "Jack, meet Allan, your new engineer."

Bill turned and left. I stood there facing Jack, who was clearly just as surprised as I was.

Jack grumbled a bit, then collected himself and bid me to follow him to my new office. I was introduced around to the other engineers in the department. I retrieved my files, bid my friends adieu, and settled into my new office.

Jack watched me work the next few weeks. He watched me carefully. Closely. Who was this kid Bill had dumped on him?

Then Jack took me to lunch. As we sat at our table he asked, "Do you know how you got this job in my department?"

"Not really."

"Well," Jack replied, "you got shoved down my throat!"

I froze for a second. I felt terrible. But Jack didn't let me hang too long. He reached his arm out and patted me on the back.

"And am I glad you did!"

"What do you mean?" I asked.

"Well, over the last few months I have interviewed numerous engineers for the opening, and none of them were a good fit. I rejected them all. I was beginning to think no one was a fit. And then there you came, out of nowhere."

He smiled. "I am thankful you are on our team. You are the right man at the right time."

From that moment on, my career took off. I did fit like a puzzle piece, working well with the team, and I was even allowed to stretch my wings. In fact, one project resulted in our team getting a patent for a steam generator. It was the place I was supposed to be, and I didn't even know it.

I have often looked back on those few seconds when I blurted out, "If I were your son, where would you want me to be?"

How did I know to say that? How did I know to let go and let God's words flow through me?

I didn't. But the Lord sure did.

QUESTIONS to inspire:

Am I willing to pause and wait for inspiration when I don't know the answer right away?

Can I decide and act spontaneously even when I lack any understanding of why?

Do I firmly believe a divine or greater power is at work for me?

Does the revealing guidance excite me when I experience it?

Any time you can listen to the true self and give it the care it requires, we do it not only for ourselves, but for the many others whose lives we touch. ~Parker palmer,

Let Your Life Speak:
Listening for the Voice of Vocation

The meaning of life... find your gift.
The purpose of life... give it away.

Chapter 7

The Ripple Effect

When we find ourselves guided by the Holy Spirit, the effects and consequences have a ripple effect. One thing leads to another, and ripples flow out from the initial event, creating profound changes in the lives of many people. This is evidence of the far-reaching value of the divine guidance that concludes each experience when Solomon's Recipe is in action.

The stories in this chapter reveal two truths of the ripple effect of the Recipe. Like a stone that is thrown into a lake and skips repeatedly across the surface, the first story shows how one result leads to another and another. The second story shows the need for patience to experience the big ripple that takes years to unfold: the long-term unexpected-consequences type of ripple effect. Actively following the Recipe will position us to affect and influence others. They will follow the Recipe without knowing it.

Father-Son Challenge

One Saturday afternoon in 1986, my wife asked me to pick up Randy, our twelve-year-old son, from the lake where he had been fishing with a friend. It was the summer after he had finished middle school and was just about to enter high school. I could see by the look in his eyes that he was waking up to the world. I had been waiting for an opportune moment to chat with him about something important.

We loaded his fishing gear into the back of my small pickup truck and headed home. On the way, when I stopped at a red light, I turned to my son.

"Randy, I want to talk to you about something. Most likely, in just a few years when you are about seventeen, you will get your driver's license. And after that, I predict that you will come home and say to me, 'Dad, will you buy me a car?' And let me tell you what my answer will be."

He looked at me expectantly. I knew that the dream of almost every young boy was to get his own car. I knew that as driving age approached, the prospect of having his own car would intensify and even monopolize every waking moment. Realizing what would soon be coursing through my son's mind, I wanted to make something very clear to him.

"My answer will be no. And it will always be no. Even if I am a millionaire by that time, I will never buy you a car." I added, "You need to think ahead and figure out how you are going to get the money to buy your own vehicle."

On the rest of the drive home, Randy's mind was racing, trying to figure out how he was going earn enough money to buy a car by the time he reached his seventeenth birthday.

The very next day, Randy approached me and begged me to take him deep-sea fishing that Monday. His target was one of the fishing boats on Point Loma. He and I had spent memorable days fishing on their half-day boats. Randy had loved fishing ever since he had caught his first fish at two years old in the surf near Rosarita Beach.

"Randy, I am working on a big project at work; I can't just take a day off right now."

He faced me, undeterred. "Well, will you take me down to the marina and let me go alone?"

"No, Randy, that's out of the question."

"Well, what if my friend Michael goes with me? Will you take the two of us then?"

Randy was bargaining hard. I think he knew I had a soft spot for Michael, since his dad had left him and his mother. I relented and asked Randy to make the proposal to Michael's mother. If she agreed, I said I would take them to the docks on Monday morning.

Randy raced out of the house and across the street to Michael's house. Minutes later, Randy and Michael came to me with the news. "Michael's mom said it's OK!"

I told the boys to get their fishing gear ready. We would need to leave at five-fifteen the next morning. I planned to send them out on a boat that left at six in the morning and returned at three-thirty in the afternoon. Carol had planned to pick them up when the boat returned.

Monday morning the boys were ready and eager to go. We packed up my pickup truck and headed to the docks. I purchased tickets for each of them and gave the boys some cash for lunch and snacks. I left them as they climbed aboard the boat and I headed off to work.

That evening at the dinner table, Randy shared his day of fishing in deep detail. His excitement was undeniable.

Then he asked, "Dad, will you take me again tomorrow?"

"Randy, I don't mind taking you there, but I can't pay twenty dollars a day for your fishing and food every day this—" But before I could finish my sentence, Randy was already responding.

"Dad, I have the money. In fact, I have twenty-six dollars, so I am covered!"

Curious, I inquired, "Randy, where did you get that kind of money?"

"Well Dad, you know how when we go fishing together, we always throw back the mackerel? Well, I saved all the mackerel Mike and I caught. Then when I got home, I filleted them and put them in plastic bags. Then, I went to all the Filipino ladies in the neighborhood and sold the cleaned fish for fifty cents each. So now I have $26."

I sat back and smiled, quite impressed with my son's resourcefulness. There was no way I would be able to turn down his request. Not only did he go fishing on Tuesday, but Wednesday as well. At the dinner table on Wednesday evening, Randy had yet another request.

"Dad, can you please call Gigi, the captain of the fishing boat? Here's her number."

With some concern, I inquired as to the reason.

"She wants me to work on the boat as a deckhand. Can I please? She said that all she needs is your approval."

After dinner I called Gigi, the captain of the La Jollan, the forty-foot fishing boat that makes daily three-quarter-day runs to the kelp beds off Point Loma.

I spoke to Gigi, who gave me all the details. But I needed to fully understand, so I asked, "Why do you want Randy to work for you, Gigi?"

"Don't you know what he's been doing?"

"I don't know anything beyond the fact that for the last three days he fished on your boat."

"Well, let me tell you. Randy caught my attention the very first day. I noticed him because he out-fished my regulars. I noticed, too, that he was courteous and respectful of those around him. On the second day, I was surprised when he quit fishing fifteen minutes early, cleaned up his gear, and stowed it away. Then, to my further surprise, he retrieved a bucket and nylon scrub broom and commenced to scrub down the boat! He had obviously watched my deckhands the first day and followed their lead. When Randy did the same thing today, I decided I just had to get this remarkable boy on my team before the competition got him!"

"Well then, he'll be there tomorrow morning."

Randy, anxiously listening to the conversation, was jumping out of his shoes in excitement.

"Thanks Dad! I can't wait till tomorrow!"

Randy worked as a deckhand on Gigi's boat throughout the summer. I drove him every morning and Carol picked him up every afternoon.

One day Carol arrived, but Randy wasn't quite done with his chores on the boat. Carol had been instructed to stay a distance down the dock. Randy didn't want anyone to know that his mother was picking him up.

As she stood off to the side, three men who had been fishing on the boat noticed Carol. They approached and asked if Randy was her son.

"Yes, he's my boy."

"So does his father own the boat?"

"No, why do you ask?"

"It's just the way he works, you know, with such dedication and expertise, we just figured his father must own the boat."

Carol smiled inwardly with delight, feeling a sense of pride in our son.

Randy worked on Gigi's boat until it retired from service a few years later. At that point he was immediately hired by another boat captain. By the time he reached driving age, he had amassed well over $7,000.

He worked Saturdays and holidays during the school year and throughout the week during summers and on school vacations. With the money he saved, Randy bought a used pickup truck. He treated it like gold.

When I look back on this part of my young son's life, what I find most revealing is that without even talking about it, without even telling him about it, my son was practicing Solomon's Recipe. It was not necessary for me to explain to Randy the Recipe. Just by living it, he got it.

QUESTIONS to inspire:

Does trusting God when I am unsure still present a challenge, or have I accepted my past experiences that show God's trustworthiness?

Am I able to quickly move to decide and act without the need for understanding?

Is accepting God's working in my life now a part of my normal way of facing life?

Does divine guidance and the success it brings embolden me with confidence for the next challenge I face?

I Remember How You Prayed

I woke up early one weekend morning and after breakfast went upstairs to my home office to catch up on some filing. When the phone rang, I looked at the screen. The number was unfamiliar. I hesitated to answer, expecting some telemarketer on the other end. Yet I felt compelled to pick up the phone and say hello before the answering machine picked up.

"Hello, Mr. Musterer."

I didn't recognize the voice. "Who is this?"

The reply came, "It's Michael."

I had no idea who it was. He didn't sound like any one of my friends named Michael. I wondered, *Is this a new marketing ploy?*

"Michael who?"

The voice responded, "Michael Radey. I lived across the street from you many years ago. I was your son Randy's childhood friend. I am now living in Florida."

The memories of my son's close friend Michael, a sweet kid with a broken family and an open heart, flooded back. I greeted him with warmth and asked him how he was doing.

"Oh, Mr. Musterer, I am not doing well at all."

"What's wrong, Michael?"

"It's my girlfriend, Jennifer. She has had cancer for many years and lately it's just gotten worse. And yesterday, well, the doctors have given up. They say she only has six weeks to live."

It hurt my heart to hear this. I could tell it was weighing heavily on Michael.

"Oh, I am so sorry. Is there anything I can do?"

Then Michael said something that really struck me.

"Well, yes. This might sound odd but, you did something one time that I never forgot."

"What do you mean?" I sat back in my chair, intrigued.

"Well, you remember when Randy and I were eight years old? You took us trout fishing in the Sierras. One morning, before we went out fishing again, we walked through the woods and you talked to us about God. I remember how you prayed. I mean, I never forgot that day and I wondered, would you pray with my girlfriend?"

For a moment I was speechless, overcome.

After a pause, I said, "Michael, I would be honored to pray with your girlfriend."

Choked up, I battled to hold back the tears, but they escaped and dropped down my cheeks and onto my keyboard.

Michael broke the silence and asked, "Mr. Musterer, can I call you back in a few minutes, so I can get my girlfriend on the phone?"

"Of course, Michael. I'll be waiting for your call."

I was shaken at the revelation that something I had done some twenty-five years before had given this young man a measure of hope in his moment of need. At the end of his rope, he saw a need to bring God into the situation, and he believed I could do it.

My mind flashed on the summer of 1981. I had invited Michael to join Randy and me on a four-day trout fishing trip. We were going to my favorite spot on Big Pine Creek, high on the eastern slopes of the Sierra Mountains. I had felt compassion for Michael. His father had left him and his mother some years before. Because he was without a dad, I wanted to include him in some father-son experiences.

Early on the day we left, the boys helped me load my pickup truck. While packing, I noticed that I had included my small travel Bible and pocket chalice with Holy Communion wafers. I paused with these items in my hands and thought, *Why am I taking these? I am going on vacation into the wilderness with two children. And Michael's faith is unknown to me.* And then, with a shrug, I packed them anyway. The boys said their goodbyes to their mothers, and we set out on the seven-hour trek to the mountain campground.

After three good days of fishing, lots of laughing and goofing around, and the warmth of evening campfires, Sunday morning dawned. We ate breakfast and cleaned up. I went to the truck to retrieve something when I noticed my Bible lying on the seat. I had forgotten all about it. I felt something urging me to do a thing I had not planned. Instead of heading out to fish, I would take the boys on a walk in the woods for an impromptu church service. I called out to them and told them we were headed out on a walk into the woods.

They grabbed their shoes and we started off under the canopy of tall trees.

Under my arm I carried my Bible, and in my pocket, the little gold chalice. Soon I found a beautiful spot, a clearing in the woods with lots of light and a fallen tree trunk.

The boys sat on the trunk and I told them we were going to have a little church service.

I prayed with the boys and spoke on the theme of the service that was being presented that day in our church back home, and together we celebrated Holy Communion. I prayed again and we returned to camp, picked up our fishing gear, and went back to fishing.

After that trip, I never gave any thought to what we had experienced with that little wilderness church service, nor had I shared it with anyone. I suspected that had I told someone, they might have leveled some criticism like, "Hey, you were on vacation! No need to push a church service on the kids out there!"

Now, some twenty-five years later, gratitude flooded my soul as I offered a prayer to God for inspiring me that day to take my Bible and then to have a service on that Sunday morning in the forest.

I left my office and went to the bedroom where my wife was still asleep. I woke her and told her what had just happened with Michael's call. We both marveled at this extraordinary development. I asked her to pray that I would be a blessing for Michael and his girlfriend. The phone rang, and I ran back to my office.

"Hello" I said.

"Mr. Musterer, this is my girlfriend, Jennifer."

"Hello Jennifer, it is so nice to meet you. Michael tells me that you are very sick, and the doctors seem to have given up hope."

Humbly and softly Jennifer answered, "Yes, that is true." I allowed myself to get very quiet, as I hoped God would speak through me.

"Jennifer, I do not know you, but I know that God knows you. I know that His love for you is beyond what you or I can understand. To Him you are worth a kingdom. He will not let any harm come to you. I also know that Michael loves you dearly and he has asked me to pray with you. Would you like that?"

"Yes, please." she said.

I proceeded to pray with Michael and Jennifer. I thanked God that He revealed to Michael that there was a source of help in Jennifer's dire situation. I acknowledged God in His omnipotence and asked for His grace and blessing on Jennifer's health. I asked that through His Holy Spirit, He would guide the hands and minds of the doctors to ensure a positive, blessed outcome for her. Finally, I thanked God for what He would do for Jennifer and asked that His perfect will for her be done.

The three of us spoke briefly and we said our goodbyes. I asked them to keep in touch about Jennifer's condition.

I continued to pray for Jennifer and Michael in the days that followed.

The next week, I received another call from Michael.

He said, "Last Sunday morning, Jennifer became seriously ill and was rushed to the hospital emergency room. She seemed near death. Her regular doctor could not be reached, so an emergency room doctor took over her care. This doctor reviewed her medical charts. What he saw caused him to immediately change her medication. Jennifer responded instantly to the new medication. So rapid and dramatic was the response that she was released from the hospital the next day. The disease went into remission and she is feeling better than she has for a long time. Thank you for your prayers."

"Michael, we must thank God, for it was His answer to our prayers that made the difference."

Thankful beyond words, I invited Michael to our church in his area.

With this experience I realized actions we take can have profound effects on people, and that these may be hidden for many years. I learned that we need to follow the impulses that God places into us, even if they don't seem necessary or appropriate in the moment. They are like seeds that take root and blossom only in God's perfect plan and meticulous timing.

I am reminded of a story of a nun who, during World War I, had a hospital where she treated wounded soldiers who fought in the war. Above the entry to her hospital were the words "Do Good and Disappear."

QUESTIONS to inspire:

Am I willing to trust God even when I am facing a strange situation?

Can I make the decision to act in the face of a new challenge that offers no level of understanding?

Can I still believe a divine or greater power continues to work for me?

Is the guidance and its consequences building greater confidence for the future? And am I willing to share it?

Too often we underestimate the power of a touch, a smile, a kind word, a listening ear, an honest compliment, or the smallest act of caring, all of which have the potential to turn a life around. ~ Leo Buscaglia

Chapter 8

HELPING OTHERS IN NEED

One of the great opportunities in life is when we are in a position to help those in need. When our natural talents and abilities are just what is needed to help someone, we find a new dimension of happiness and purpose. Solomon's Recipe can have a significant impact on our willingness and capability to help others. When we trust God and can follow the inspiring guidance of the Holy Spirit, we will experience some of the most extraordinary and exciting times of our life, meeting some of the most wonderful people and forming the most rewarding relationships.

Depression

I have always been blessed with a positive attitude. From a very early age, my mother's notes in her journals attested to my positive persona. I think I owe it all to her. In countless moments of uncertainty and doubt, I witnessed her unwavering and relentless positivity. She was a woman of deep faith and she gave me a touchstone, an outlook on life that helped me face my own moments of fear and uncertainty. Using that tool of positivity had always worked for me. Until the day it didn't.

I found myself suddenly and unexpectedly gripped in a deep depression. I was in my mid-forties. I was happily married with a son we adored. In the past, as a minister and engineer, I had been a useful, needed soul. As I looked over my life, I found there was no particularly upsetting situation I was facing, so I wondered, *Why do I feel so heavy, so hopeless, so helpless?*

Daily I prayed and sought divine understanding. Day after day I awoke with a feeling and sense of being so sad and very hopeless. My growing feeling of depression became more and more disconcerting. Nothing I tried was working.

But I couldn't give up. So, I tried even harder to dispel this nagging sense of gloom invading me. I attempted to think of positive aspects of my life. I prayed again and again, asking God to remove this thorn in my side. I looked at my family and thought that my appreciation for the blessing they are for me would do the trick. But alas, not even that worked. With no hope for a way out, the depression deepened a little more each day.

One Sunday morning I decided I needed to try something new as I was preparing to go to church. I was to conduct the sermon and felt that God would surely remove this pain to enable me to serve the congregation. When the time came, I got up, delivered the sermon to the best of my ability, and then sat down. I waited. Nothing was changing. Nothing had left me, and my depression weighed more heavily on my chest.

That night I researched depression. I found out that there are two basic types of depression: clinical depression and emotional (or situational) depression. Both are detrimental to a person's mental health and overall happiness. Clinical depression is a bit more serious and is caused by chemical imbalances in the brain. It requires professional medical and psychiatric attention. Emotional depression, on the other hand, may be resolved in another way. I felt I was experiencing the second kind of depression but didn't know my way out. I wondered, *What is the solution to my situation?*

On Monday morning I awoke, my pain deeper than ever, prompted by my failures to escape it. All I wanted was to stay in bed. Yet I willed myself, with every ounce of strength left, to get ready for work. I dressed and had breakfast and made my way out the door. I was rattled and unnerved. I was afraid. I tried to pray but the words were a struggle and I felt I didn't reach my God. I was empty.

Along the two-mile route to my office, at every traffic light I encountered, I wondered, *What will I do? What can I do? Haven't I exercised every option?*

I drove under a freeway overpass, and as I approached an on-ramp (one that I don't take to work) for the freeway going north, I experienced an intense feeling of wanting to just drive onto the ramp. I felt a pull I could not explain to just drive away from everyone and everything and never return. Thoughts swirled, like *Maybe I have outlived my usefulness in the world. Maybe I am not needed anymore.* I had to fight hard not to get on that freeway, and instead I forced myself to drive to work. I sat in my car outside my office and realized that I had to take some drastic action, and that it had to happen now.

As I got out of my car, a thought came. *There is one person who can help me. My dear friend Alex. He's always upbeat and positive. He will help me see a way out.*

Alex was my mentor and I'd had great respect for him for many years. Like me, he had a reputation of having a deep faith and an unusually positive perspective. He would be a light for me in this devastating darkness as he had always been. As I dialed, I felt a twinge of hope.

When Alex answered the phone, I poured my heart out to him. I confided that I couldn't see a current situation that was causing this, but whatever was at its root, it was getting worse by the hour.

After I finished my lament, I waited, expecting to hear his bright shiny voice say, "Allan, I understand. I assure you; all will be well with you. Let's pray together." And from there I thought that my problem would be solved.

But to my shock and surprise, there was a long, almost deafening silence. I anxiously awaited his response. What I heard Alex say was something that I never expected.

He simply said, "Allan, me too."

In the silence that followed, thoughts whirled around in my head. *What? My best friend is battling such depression too? How can that be? He is my paragon of positivity! Where's my, 'Allan I understand; let's pray and all will be well?' What now?*

I was speechless, pondering what I just heard. Alex broke the silence.

Softly he said, "But, I'll make you a deal. If you'll pray for me, I'll pray for you."

That statement pierced my soul like a burning arrow. Maybe I wasn't useless. Then, to my great surprise, I found my whole perspective begin to shift. My focus on my negative feelings was replaced, and I instantly embraced my new mission—praying for my best friend. I quickly agreed and ended the call.

With new direction and urgency I raced to the men's room, locked the door, and in privacy I prayed intently for my friend Alex and his struggle with depression. When I finally said my "Amen," I realized that my depressed feelings had suddenly vanished. I was amazed and confounded as to what had just transpired. I wondered, *How and why this sudden and unexpected change? What is going on?*

I returned to my office and pondered what I had just experienced. As I did so, I soon realized what Alex had done. By expressing the very simple "Me too," he engaged me. Then, he wisely and deliberately waited, giving my mind time in the silence to process the fact that my dear friend needed my help. Then, he opened the door for me to help him. He created in me the realization that he needed me now. Not only did he need me, but he acknowledged that I had the ability to help him and that in prayer there was hope for both of us.

How simple, yet profound, our conversation had been. I took this moment of discovery to pause and thank God for opening this precious moment of new understanding. Finally, I had found peace. I wondered why God had brought me through this experience.

Suddenly, I recalled a meeting I'd had with Alex in his office many months before. Sitting at his desk, my eyes were drawn to a plaque mounted on the wall that read "PRAYER CHANGES THINGS." Smiling, I thought, *Yes, and prayer changes me!*

A few weeks later, I received a phone call from someone who had been a member in our church but had moved away. She was suffering from intense feelings of worry, anxiety, and sadness.

"Allan, I am deeply concerned for my children. I feel so helpless, hopeless, and unwanted. There seems to be a darkness about me. What can I do? Please help me. I can't get over this feeling. It's possible that I may be seriously depressed."

I took a moment, had a quick smile with God, and said, "Yes, my dear friend, me too."

Then after a deliberate pause, I posed the same deal.

"If you'll pray for me, I'll pray for you."

"Oh no! You too? I'll definitely pray for you."

"And I'll pray for you."

A few days later, she called again and shared with me her experience of how our conversation and our prayers lightened her feelings, that her depression was lifting, and that she felt more equipped to handle the issues facing her.

I sat back and mused. I thought, *None of us, though we may feel this way from time to time, are useless or unwanted. How simple, yet profound, the act of praying for one another—of knowing we are not in this alone—can be.*

QUESTIONS to inspire:

Am I willing to trust God when I am completely at a loss with a new situation and no history on which to draw?

Can I actively move forward without a shred of understanding what is happening?

Do I place my belief and trust that divine and greater power is at work for me?

When I see the successful results of the experienced guidance, am I willing to share it with others?

A Dying Soul Finds Peace

In April 2015, my brother-in-law became seriously ill. Carol and I immediately booked a flight to New Jersey. Daily we visited the hospice hospital, supporting his children's bedside vigil.

The day after he passed, Carol and her brother's adult children went to her brother's house to retrieve some legal documents. I stayed at home with Karen, a member of the extended family who had come to watch the younger children while their parents were taking care of details for the funeral.

As we drank coffee in the kitchen, I could tell she was bearing a heavy weight. "You know," she began, "I find it very easy to talk with you."

"That's very kind of you." I could tell she was hesitating. "Karen, it's okay. What's on your mind?"

"Well, it's my dad. His health is failing. And he's not someone that I would say is at peace with himself."

"Why do you think that is?" I asked.

"Strained relationships with some family members. I feel so helpless to offer him comfort. Would you mind praying for him? His name is Harold Haas."

I immediately agreed and prayed for Harold often during the weeks that followed.

A few months later, while we were visiting our relatives, Karen asked if I might visit her dad. Harold's health had deteriorated to the point that Karen had moved him into her home, where she hoped he might find some comfort. I could see by the look in her eyes that she worried her father was a man who was still not at peace.

At Karen's home, we were given a tour of the grounds. It was a very old house with a large barn, lots of lush nature, tall trees, and a beautiful stream that ran through the property. After the tour, Karen took us to Harold, who was seated on the sofa in the living room. Bundled up in a sweat suit and knitted beanie, it was obvious he was very weak. When he spoke, his words were painful, labored. I thought it better not to try to talk with him further, but we shared a meaningful glance. He saw I cared.

I turned away from Harold and noticed extraordinary oil paintings of nature hanging on the living room walls. Trees and brooks, rocks and flowers, big blue skies and low hanging clouds. I gazed in awe, moving from one painting to the next. The trees and flowers were so lifelike, they looked more like photographs than paintings. When I finally caught my breath, I remarked that the paintings were quite impressive.

"They were all painted by Harold," Karen said, and then she asked me if I would sit with her dad for a few minutes, as she had to make an important phone call. I gladly agreed to sit with Harold, yet I wondered what to say. I again surveyed the room, taking in the amazing collection of paintings adorning the walls.

As I studied the art created at the hands of Harold, it became clear to me, a fellow artist, that Harold possessed an extraordinary God-given gift for replicating the fine points of Creation. He made it feel intimate, as if you were standing at the base of the oak tree, gazing up at the leaves that were blowing in the wind.

"Harold, what inspired you to take up painting?"

His voice was barely a whisper. "My wife suggested I take up a hobby when I retired."

"But how did you learn to harness your natural talent?"

"I'm not exactly sure. I think I just practiced and practiced till I got it right."

I imagined he invested much time and energy to achieve such mastery. Then suddenly, his voice became stronger and he said, "I found I could only paint if the painting had a destination, a home . . . like these here, for my daughter."

That unexpected statement caused me to stop and think. Harold's gift came to life when the purpose of his painting was to be a blessing for someone else. This struck me as an amazing legacy. All the paintings in that room were destined for his daughter Karen.

The conversation about the paintings opened Harold's heart and strengthened his voice. No longer struggling, he spoke with firm resolve. I listened as he poured out his heart with issues that troubled him and stole his peace of mind. These words will forever remain only with me. Yet I can say that what he revealed showed me that he was a kind, understanding, and quite extraordinary man. He was willing and able to forgive others, no matter the hurt they may have caused. I was humbled by his generosity of spirit.

When Karen returned to the room, I offered to pray with them. Karen and Harold welcomed my invitation. In my prayer I asked God to bless Harold with the peace he had lost, in the way that only the Lord can provide.

I took my leave of Harold and his family, feeling blessed myself for our interaction.

I marveled at how God had employed my appreciation for art to open a door for Harold and me to come together. I cherished those few moments I shared with him and hoped they would continue to bless him.

Shortly after I returned home, I received word that Harold had passed on. Karen wrote to me, saying that she really believed I was meant to be there to help her dad that day. She said that after I left, an inner calm had washed over her father. It was a calm she had not seen for quite a long time. She saw, both in his eyes and in his spirit, that her father was finally at peace.

Questions to inspire

Am I willing to trust God when I am at a loss facing a new situation?

Can I actively move forward without understanding what is expected of me?

Do I believe and trust that divine power will again come to help me?

When I see the successful results of God's guidance, am I willing to share it with others?

The Rice Conspiracy

In 1980, a large group of Hmong refugee families became members of our church. One of the many things we did to assist our families from Southeast Asia was to educate them in the art of buying food at the local supermarket. Since many of them did not have cars yet, most of their shopping was limited to the one local supermarket that was within walking distance. During one evening at a pastoral visit to the Cha family, one of the largest families, I asked, "What is your biggest challenge?"

I expected talk of cultural differences, fitting in, or maybe finding work. But when the man of the house spoke up, his response surprised me.

"Well, our problem is rice. You see, rice is part of every meal for us. We eat a lot of rice. When we arrived here, we could buy a 100-pound sack of our favorite rice for about twenty dollars at the local market. But now the price has been doubled. It is over forty dollars. We cannot afford this, and many are struggling. Is there anything you can do?"

I was taken aback. I explained that this was a subject unfamiliar to me but said I would investigate. I also explained that I would pray to see what solution God might inspire to help us solve this dilemma. I left the house wondering how in the world I would tackle this rice problem.

That night, I prayed for God's guidance. I had never faced anything close to this type of dilemma before, and I honestly had no idea what to do. I was a bit stumped. I needed divine intervention, or at least some measure of understanding as to what to do first.

The next day while at work, I related the dilemma of the refugees to a co-worker. His eyes lit up. "I think I have an idea."

Within moments, he put me in touch with an acquaintance of his who was a food distributor. I called, introduced myself, and explained the situation. He asked me for a more precise description of the kind of rice. I described the white sack with a large red rose and yellow lettering I saw at the Cha apartment. He said he thought he could be of some help.

When my lunch hour arrived, I went to the neighborhood where our church members lived. I parked my car in the lot of the one and only supermarket. I entered the store and made my way to the aisle that contained the bulk rice. I quickly noticed the 100-pound rice sacks. The price was forty-two dollars each.

I made my way to the checkout counter and asked to see the store manager. The checker got on the phone, and a few minutes later the manager appeared. He was a smug man with little patience. I could tell he was annoyed that I had asked for him.

"How can I help you?"

I responded, "Sir, I have a concern. Would you mind coming with me to the bulk rice aisle?"

At the aisle I pointed out the 100-pound sack of rice with the red rose on it. "I suspect you sell a lot of these?"

"Oh yes! Those are my best seller! The locals buy that brand the most."

"Yes, that's what I've heard. I also understand that a few months ago, you sold this bag for $19.99, but now it's over $40. Was there a reason that you needed to increase the price? For instance, did the wholesale price increase?"

He responded with wry smile. "No. In fact, I am getting a better deal because I sell so many."

I could feel my blood boil. He was taking advantage of them and he knew it. I tried to sound calm and clear as I spoke.

"Sir, did you know that many Asian refugees have just moved into this neighborhood and that many of them are struggling to make ends meet? Rice is their staple and what you are doing is price gouging."

The manager looked at me in defiance. I continued. "I'm going to say something that will not make you happy. You have twenty-four hours to reduce the price to the original $19.99 or I guarantee you will never sell another bag of that rice."

With a tone of arrogance, he replied, "And who are you?"

"Well, I guess you will discover that tomorrow when I show up to see if you have complied with my challenge to do the right thing."

He turned in a huff and marched off. I left the store and returned to work.

I called the food distributor I had spoken to earlier in the day and gave him more detailed specifications of the rice. After a few moments he told me he could deliver 200 or more of the 100-pound sacks of rice for twelve dollars per sack.

The following day, I anxiously awaited my lunch break. As soon as the clock turned twelve, I left for the supermarket. Entering the front door, I made my way to the bulk rice aisle. As I anticipated, the price was unchanged from the previous day. Once again, I summoned the manager.

When he arrived, he shot me a look of arrogance; if possible, he was even more smug than the day before.

"Oh! It's you. And how can I help you today?"

"Well, to be honest, I am disappointed that you have not done the right thing for the families in this neighborhood. Any chance you might reconsider and lower the price right here and now?"

He smirked, turned, and walked away without a word.

I left the market and went to see the Cha family. I explained my plan to provide rice at a competitive price. They were thrilled and agreed with my plan. I returned to work.

Once at the office, I called the food distributor. I placed an order for 300 sacks of rice to be delivered to the Chas' address. The food distributor informed me that they would arrive in two days. Arrangements were made for the Chas to get the word out to our church members. The plan called for them to distribute one or two sacks per family at twelve dollars each. Friends and neighbors who were not members of the church could buy one per family at fifteen dollars each. My rationale was the extra money for non-members would be given to the Chas for storing the excess rice in their home and managing the distribution.

Two days later, I received a call that a semi-truck would arrive at eleven that morning. I had already made the $3600 payment via a bank transfer and left work early to meet the truck just outside the Chas' apartment. I was amazed to see about a dozen Hmong men standing there, waiting to help with the unloading.

The truck rolled up and parked right on time. The unloading proceeded with one sack after another hoisted on the men's sturdy shoulders. They carried them into the Chas' apartment and stacked them up against a wall. I watched in awe as bag after bag left the back of the truck on the way to the apartment for storage and distribution. The scene reminded me of movies that depicted the building of the Egyptian pyramids with a multitude of people carrying building materials in a continuous stream of manpower.

With amazing efficiency, members of the Cha family were keeping tally. Within a half hour they began distribution to the nearby church members and their neighbors.

When the last bag was removed from the trailer, the driver had me sign a document and off he went.

I returned to the Cha home and surveyed the situation. About 150 sacks had already been distributed, with the remainder stacked to the ceiling of the Chas' living room. I told them to hold on to the money and give me the $3600 when it was collected. The extra was for the "cost" of storing and was to remain with the family. The whole experience left me with an overwhelming feeling of gratitude and awe. I thought about what a community can do when it comes together.

A week later, I returned to the supermarket. I took a stroll down the bulk rice aisle only to see that rice with the red rose was still at forty-two dollars. Again, I searched out the manager. He arrived with a scowl.

"Have you sold any 100-pound sacks of rice lately?"

He wouldn't answer.

"Well, if you lower the price to where it was originally, you might again find willing buyers. But you might have to go down to fifteen dollars a sack to get back to the volume you had previously achieved."

With a look of disdain, he turned and left.

Ultimately, by the time our supply of rice ran out, the manager had lowered the price.

I looked back to the moment when I had absolutely no idea how to solve this problem. And yet, somehow, resources appeared, and a path was created. This experience revealed that there is truth to the adage, "Where there's a will, there's a way." Especially after a prayer.

What mission awaits you? Do you believe you can do it? If so, you will find a way!

Questions to inspire

When facing a new challenge, am I willing to trust God's support?

Can I truly believe that God will actively help me move forward without my understanding?

Will my belief that divine power will again come to help me be enough to get past any lingering doubts?

When I see the successful results of God's guidance, am I willing to share it with others?

If Plan A didn't work, keep cool.
The alphabet has twenty-five more letters,
And Plan G will finally be the perfect
solution, because it's God's perfect plan
for you and your situation.

CHAPTER 9

Soul Growth and Self-Care

When a loved one suffers from dementia or Alzheimer's disease or has a stroke, you may find yourself in a care-giving situation. This is seldom planned, so you are probably uninformed and uneducated as to what to expect and how to cope with experiencing someone so dear to you suffering and in need of special care. Emotions are high, and as caregiver, you can find yourself doubting your capacity to cope. Although classes provided by social services are welcome and effective, it remains for you to do the work of caring for a loved one. Likewise, when God steps in at any circumstance of life and shows you He is near and helping, you need to acknowledge it and keep it alive as a daily resource.

Mother's Debilitating Stroke

My mother and I have always shared a powerful spiritual bond. From my earliest days, my mother was an immense blessing, having saved my life on more than one occasion. So, when she suffered a major stroke which left her paralyzed and struggling with her memory and recognition, it hit me hard. In fact, I can say I may have never experienced a pain so deep. I felt helpless. As if I could not do enough. So much so, that at times I felt paralyzed.

And yet, my deep trust in the Lord revealed an extraordinary insight, one that would rescue me from the depths of pain that gripped my heart.

One Sunday morning, my wife, son, parents, and I journeyed down the freeway to attend our morning church service. In my mind, I was prepping for the sermon I would be giving within the hour.

Just before the service began, as I was still ruminating about just the right word choice for my sermon, a member of our church rushed up to me with a look of panic. He took my hand and said that my mother had suddenly collapsed in her seat. I flew to her side. When I saw her, I noticed the telltale signs of a stroke. My mother's face was distorted, her jaw was slack, and she could barely move the left side of her body. In a panic I shouted out for someone to call 911.

Within a few minutes an ambulance arrived, and my confused mother was placed on a stretcher and whisked away. My dad, a tight knot of worry, jumped into the ambulance to ride with her.

I remained behind and conducted the most difficult sermon of my life. It was hard to concentrate, as my heart had left when my mother did. Immediately after the service, I rushed to the hospital. I found my father in a waiting room. He was discussing Mom's condition with a neurosurgeon.

"She needs immediate surgery. She has suffered an aneurism and is bleeding in the right side of her brain."

We stood for a moment in shock.

"We need your consent."

My father found his voice. "Yes, of course. Yes. You have my consent."

As the surgeon rushed off, we made our way to a little chapel. It was empty when we entered and I immediately prayed with my dad. I prayed that the doctors would be guided by God's Spirit to serve the best for my mother. Then we left for uncomfortable blue seats in the waiting room. We stayed there the entire day until the sun went down and the surgeon walked in to tell us that she was out of surgery.

"How did it go?" my father asked.

"Good," he reassured us. "As well as can be expected. She will be fine. All her faculties should return to normal within a few days or weeks. You can go see her when you are ready."

We rushed into the recovery room to find her awake and coherent, a large white bandage circling her head. She remembered our names. I sighed in relief. Then she said, "Oh and please don't forget to mail the birthday cards that are supposed to go out tomorrow. We don't want them to show up late." My father and I shared a smile.

Though we were initially encouraged, her health declined after we took her home. She was experiencing complications from the surgery, and the rehabilitation did not improve her condition. They began giving her heavy medications. At its worst, my mother began experiencing brain seizures. Her body was struggling, and her mental state was as well. We had no choice but to place her in a special care facility. The decision weighed heavily on both my father and me, but we knew her needs were beyond what we could provide at home.

During the week prior to my dad passing on, he and I visited my mother in the evening. As we approached, she looked up at us from her wheelchair, confused and clearly in a medicated fog.

"Eddy, is that you?"

"Yes dear, it's me," Dad replied

Then looking at me, she asked, "Who are you?"

"It's Allan," I said.

"Oh."

We didn't speak much more on that visit. My heart sank. I knew she couldn't really process who I was, which broke my heart.

When I visited alone, she often mistook me for my father or my brother. Even though I understood the cause, each time she failed to recognize me, it gripped my heart.

However, God was at work in ways I could not see at the time.

Each Sunday after conducting the morning church service in one of the San Diego area congregations under my care, I took whatever detour necessary to stop at the convalescent home. I wanted to serve my mother with Absolution and Holy Communion, and to pray with her. I held a living hope that despite her condition, somehow these blessings of God would reach her soul.

One Sunday when I walked into the entrance of the convalescent home, the first thing I saw was my mother in her wheelchair. She was first in the line of wheelchairs at the entry to the dining hall. She was hunched over, her eyeglasses askew and smudged to the point that she could barely see. I entered the large reception room from the foyer and Mother immediately looked up, raised her "good" right arm, and called out my name.

"Allan! Is that you?" she said with a strong voice that all could hear. Her voice was slurred but still strong. I helped clear her eyeglasses.

I responded, "Yes, it's me."

Mother, again calling out so loud the whole room could hear, said, "Do you have my Holy Communion?"

"Yes, I do, Mother."

I gave her a kiss and wheeled her back to her room.

In the privacy of her room, I shared highlights of the morning church service. I spoke to her as though there was nothing wrong with her comprehension. We prayed the Lord's Prayer, and to my amazement, she prayed that prayer as though nothing was wrong with her! Every word was correct and there was no slurred speech. She prayed as if she was a fully healthy person.

I followed the Lord's Prayer with pronouncement of the Absolution and served her Holy Communion. Finally, I pronounced the Benediction.

We said "Amen" together and mother looked up at me and said, "Who are you?"

My heart sank. I found the words to speak. "I'm Allan, your son."

"Oh. Is it time for lunch?"

"Yes, Mother, I'm taking you there now."

I released the brakes on the wheelchair and took Mother to the now-filled dining room for lunch. I kissed her and said goodbye as a mixture of feelings, mostly sadness and angst, flooded my soul.

The next Sunday, almost the exact scene was duplicated. She recognized me, and her speech was slurred until the moment she prayed, when it became crystal clear. Then at times she failed to recognize me by the end of the visit.

The first few times I had this experience, I left my mother deeply saddened.

Yet after my third or fourth visit with this same experience, I realized that God was showing me something very important. As I left the facility it was clear to me.

Even though her body and mind were in peril, broken even, her soul remained perfectly healthy and strong.

This insight filled me with gratitude and bathed me in the comfort I had been seeking. God was reaching out to me with the unwavering message that though the body might fail, the soul never will.

~

Have you experienced that when your emotions overwhelmed you, you missed seeing God's actions resolving your concern?

Questions to inspire

Can I sincerely trust God when I am in deep pain and disappointment with the necessity of facing new situation?

Can I actively move forward without understanding what is expected of me?

Do I believe and trust that divine power will again come to help me reach a good outcome?

When I see the successful results of the God's guidance, am I willing to share it with others?

Dementia

When it became apparent that Clara, my mother-in-law, needed more care than was available to her in New Jersey, we knew it was time to move her home with us. She had been struggling with dementia for a few years and it was clear that she was in decline.

Shortly after her arrival, she insisted on living in her own place, so we found nice assisted living facility just a short drive from our home. Clara's dementia was mild at first, revealed in her lack of short-term memory. Other than that, she was quite witty and physically healthy. Soon, however, she became prone to falling, and that necessitated frequent trips to the emergency room.

Clara and I dealt with her dementia with humor by teasing one another playfully. It became a game for us that subdued the sadness of Clara's memory challenges. We started this joking around because she would ask the same question over and over. We agreed she could ask a given question five times per day. By the sixth time, Carol and I didn't have to answer. Clara took to this kind of joking around, sometimes messing with our heads for a good laugh.

One evening, Carol, Clara and I were watching a TV show. Clara sat in her recliner while Carol and I sat on the sofa. Our cat Scarlett sat on Carol's lap. Suddenly, Clara left her chair and pushed her walker toward the bathroom.

"I'll be right back," she said.

About twenty minutes later, Clara appeared in the bathroom doorway, looking puzzled, as if she didn't recognize anyone or anything.

I sat up, abruptly pointed at her, and said, "Do I know you?"

She replied, "Well, we could get acquainted!" Again, I saw that wry look on her face that said, "Gotcha!"

Carol and I burst into hysterical laughter. Lighthearted moments like these helped ease the monotony and pain of watching our dear mother decline.

On another occasion, during a visit with relatives from New Jersey, I went to pick up Clara to bring her to our house for dinner. Twice before, I had told her who would be visiting.

I was stopped at a traffic light when Mom spoke up.

"Allan. Now who is coming for dinner?"

"Mom, that's the fourth time you asked me that question."

"No, it isn't! It's the third time. Just so you know, I'm counting too!"

Tears welled up in my eyes as I battled a fit of uncontrolled laughter. When I arrived at home, I shared Mom's latest quip, bringing everyone into the lighthearted moment.

One time I was scheduled to take Clara to a rehabilitation facility for physical therapy. I entered her room and announced that we were going to rehab. She arose and headed to the bathroom. A few minutes later she emerged, looked up at me and asked, "Where are we going?"

"We are going to rehab."

"Oh, okay."

We walked down the hall to the elevator. While waiting, just as expected, she questioned me again.

"Where are we going?" she said, looking at me with big, hopeful eyes.

"We are going to rehab."

"Oh! Okay."

Once on the main floor we exited the elevator and walked toward the front door. Clara stopped and looked up at me, again with those hope-filled eyes.

"Where are we going?"

"We are going to rehab."

"Oh! Okay."

We walked outside and to the car, Clara slowly pushing her walker. I opened the passenger side door and helped her in, then folded up her walker and put it into the trunk. I got in behind the wheel. She looked over at me expectantly and was about to speak, when I interrupted.

"Mom, you just asked that question three times. According to our agreement, you have only two left. Are you sure you want to ask it again now?"

"Well, how long is it going to take to get to where we are going?" she inquired.

"Why do you want to know?"

"Because I want to be sure there will be enough time to use them up!" she quipped.

I burst into uncontrolled laughter. I sat there for five minutes or more, the tears running down my face, laughing at Clara's sharp wit and humor.

She looked at me with a sly grin, relishing the moment she sent me into stitches.

By keeping a sense of humor, I was able to maintain and even enjoy my relationship with Clara. The humor was able to assuage, to some degree, the emotional anguish for both me and Carol as we witnessed Clara's diminished capacity evolve.

When this situation with Clara began, my only experience with someone with seriously diminished memory was with my mother. She'd had a debilitating stroke, and the lack of memory was a very painful experience. I hoped it wouldn't be the same with Clara. Exercising Solomon's Recipe, I prayed for guidance as to how or what I could do to make the relationship with Clara more pleasant for me and Carol. I watched for some indication of guidance from above. That's when Clara's first humorous quip opened the door to humor and playful teasing.

Questions to inspire:

Am I willing to trust God when I am struggling to deal with a new and deeply personal situation?

Can I, without understanding what is expected of me, still trustingly follow guidance when it comes?

Do I trust that divine power will again come to help me, or am I still wrestling with doubt?

When I see the successful results of God's guidance, am I willing to share it with others?

The Helicopter Incident ~
Remembering the Hand of God

Anthony and Cindy, a warm Navy couple from the eastern United States, were transferred to San Diego in 2000. They joined our congregation soon after their arrival. After our first service, they came to shake my hand. Anthony smiled wide and brought greetings from my cousin Cliff, who had been their minister in the congregation they attended back east.

As we spoke, I immediately liked this man. I could tell he was humble, dedicated, and sincere. About a year later, when he shared with me that he was about to be deployed overseas, I had mixed feelings.

Anthony would be responsible for the maintenance of the helicopter squadron assigned to his carrier. I knew it was his duty and he was ready to go, yet I also knew that his deployment would be taking him to a war zone in the Middle East. Tony came to see me before he left. I could see he was worried, both for himself and for his wife and two children.

I did my best to find the right words. "Tony, be assured that I will be praying for you and your team as you embark on this mission. I will also keep the congregation praying for you. I am sure our almighty God will be with you at every moment. Know that His powerful hand will guide you."

He responded with a grateful, "Thank you." He then asked if we might be able to stay in touch via email, since he would have occasional internet access. I immediately agreed. "That will be great, let's do that."

When he sent his emails during the months of his absence, he couldn't mention his location, but I did know he was in a war zone, and as such, would be facing moments when his life was in jeopardy.

Our daily prayers always included him and the situation his work entailed.

One day I received an email from Anthony that caused me to immediately offer a heartfelt prayer of thanksgiving. He shared a very special event for him which became a very special moment for me:

> *Dear Evangelist,*
>
> *Please tell the congregation family to keep praying for me and my shipmates, because it is working. I must tell you what happened. One of our helicopters needed maintenance. My crew worked on it and finalized the required actions and advised me it was ready for my inspection. I climbed up on the helicopter to survey their work, making sure everything was done according to specification. Then suddenly, when I moved to take a step, I lost my footing. I slid down the front face of the helicopter, precariously heading for the drink. Because the ship was underway, falling into the sea would almost surely be fatal. Then, just as suddenly as I fell, I*

stopped sliding for no apparent reason. I had not snagged onto any part of the helicopter. My astonished crew immediately came to my rescue. As I considered what had just happened, I realized it had to be the hand of God that stopped me from sliding off the copter and into the sea. I am so grateful. So please, ask the congregation to keep praying!

I related Anthony's story to the congregation that Sunday, and they all agreed to continue their prayerful support of our brother.

It was quite some time later, following Anthony's return home, that we were able to talk in person. During our conversation, Anthony questioned whether God was with him on his journey, because he felt he faced many obstacles and at times he felt alone.

"But Anthony, you know without doubt that God is with you!"

His response surprised me when he said, "Why do you say that, how should I know?"

"Well, the helicopter incident is the evidence."

"What helicopter incident?"

Anthony's puzzled look told me he must have forgotten the experience that had so deeply touched his life and mine.

I reminded Anthony of the incident that he had shared with me in that email so many months before.

He shook his head and smiled wide in remembrance. "Oh yes, that was awesome; I had forgotten all about it."

"Anthony, you can't forget something so powerful. You need to share that with the world. I must confess, I have told your story since then maybe a hundred times. How many times have you shared that amazing experience?"

"I only told it once, in that email to you," he confessed.

"Oh Tony, you have to tell that story. That's your story with God. He had a purpose for that story. God expects you to tell it. I believe that story will help countless others."

"Okay, I'll do it," he said, with a renewed sense of purpose.

~

Sometimes we experience a moment in time when God touches our life in a unique and special way. It deeply moves our soul. But then, life with all its noise can drown out our sense of awe. Slowly our experience slips away and out of our thoughts. We forget it, and its power of transforming us and others departs. Its purpose has been lost. We need to remember these life-changing moments by sharing them with others, thereby keeping them alive within our hearts.

Sharing your stories magnifies the magic and can spark a sense of hope, healing, or awe. You never know who might need to hear your story today.

Questions to inspire

Am I willing to trust God when I think I know what to do but harbor the feeling I could be wrong?

Can I still move forward without understanding what I need to say or do?

Do I see that divine power will again come to help me, even with smaller issues?

When I see the success of God's guidance, am I willing to share it with others?

A grateful heart is one that finds the countless blessings in their life, no matter their situation.

Don't be ashamed of your story, and don't forget it either. Tell it proudly, because it will be an inspiration to someone else.

CHAPTER 10

How to Make the Most of Your Experiences

Write Your Experiences Down When They Happen

As you go through the dynamic experience of living life by Solomon's Recipe, do your best to capture your thoughts in real time. How do you do this? Just grab a journal and put down any and all thoughts about your experiences. Remember this is just for you, so don't worry about spelling or grammar. Feel free to capture everything you are thinking and feeling. This kind of journaling can have multiple effects. First, you will capture thoughts, ideas, doubts, insights, and revelations that may otherwise pass you by. Second, you may uncover fine details that were overlooked or hidden from your consciousness as the events happened. Third, by keeping this journal, you will be able to relive your experiences at a later date. You may be the person to inspire yourself as you reread your entries.

Three Steps to Allow Communication with God

1. Pay attention to the unexpected, which can come in any of these forms:
   - ☐ thoughts
   - ☐ feelings
   - ☐ dreams
   - ☐ meetings
   - ☐ messages (from art, movies, plays, books, Bible)
   - ☐ coincidences
   - ☐ events
   - ☐ answers (from strangers, friends, clergy)
   - ☐ triggers (smells, sights, sounds)

2. Play the waiting game by interacting with the Lord.
As you wait and watch for what is coming next, use the time to ask the following questions:

   - Am I being prepared for a situation that is yet to come?
   - Am I being taught something that I need to know?
   - Am I being guided to a place where I need to be?
   - Am I being put in a position to help someone else?

- Am I being shown something that I need to understand?

3. Seek out a completion to your experience.

After you think that your situation has concluded, ask these questions:
- Is there something else?
- Is this message for me or for someone else?
- What do I do with this? How do I put this into motion?

This is a wonderful time to turn to prayer and ask, "Please help me see what You need me to see, so that Your purpose can be fulfilled."

Practice, Practice, Practice

The more you think of Solomon's Recipe as a practice rather than a destination, the more impact it will have in your life. Further, you will begin to feel the compounding impact of ongoing practice. The more trust you give, the more guidance you will receive. Each time you witness Solomon's Recipe working for you, the more you will believe it. Every experience will prepare you for the next. You will be quicker to remind yourself of the lessons you have learned, and you will be rewarded with unfolding layers of understanding.

Share Your Story—Maybe Write a Book?

As you build your library of Solomon's Recipe experiences, you may begin to appreciate that maybe, just maybe, these experiences were not just for you. When the time is right and you feel ready, tell your story to others. Share your insights and revelations.

Consider that, as powerful as your experiences were for you, they may hold the same transformative power for someone else. A relative, a friend, a classmate, a teacher, a student, or even a total stranger may need to hear your story at just the moment that you are ready to share it. Imagine, your telling just one story to one person who then retells that story to two people, and within a short time over a million will hear it and be blessed by it. Now that's powerful.

Appendix

Provocative questions to inspire your growth as you practice the Recipe:

- Why have I assumed trust was not possible?
- Why do I still insist on understanding?
- Why can't I take a leap?
- How am I impatient?
- Why can't I give credit elsewhere?
- Why can't I see guidance from outside of me?
- How can I practice the Recipe daily?

Create a Solomon's Recipe Circle of Friendship (or Circle of Support)

My Prayer

Almighty God, I come to you with a grateful heart, thankful for Your grace, Your mercy, Your love, Your guidance, and all the good You bring to my life. Such thanksgiving is beyond the words I know, so I invite You to search my heart to see what I cannot say. I pray that You would make me a blessing to someone today. Give me a heart with the skill and sensitivity to hear Your Holy Spirit when He whispers His guidance. Give me the courage to act and the words to speak to fulfill Your purpose in that person's life. Amen

The following are various translations of Solomon's Recipe

These are provided because sometimes one can find a very personal connection to specific words that a translator might use to express a notion or idea. This can give additional meaning and depth to how you see and appreciate the Recipe.

Proverbs 3:5–6 The Passion Translation (TPT)

Wisdom's Guidance

5 Trust in the Lord completely,
and do not rely on your own opinions.
With all your heart rely on him to guide you,
and he will lead you in every decision you make.
6 Become intimate with him in whatever you do,
and he will lead you wherever you go.

Proverbs 3:5–6 The Voice (VOICE)

5 Place your trust in the Eternal; *rely on Him* completely;
 never depend upon your own ideas and inventions.
6 Give Him the credit for everything you accomplish,
and He will *smooth out and* straighten the road that lies ahead.

Proverbs 3:5–6 The Living Bible (TLB)

4-5 If you want favor with both God and man, and a reputation for good judgment and common sense, then trust the Lord completely; don't ever trust yourself. 6 In everything you do, put God first, and he will direct you and crown your efforts with success.

Proverbs 3:5–6 Good News Translation (GNT)

5 Trust in the LORD with all your heart. Never rely on what you think you know. 6 Remember the LORD in everything you do, and he will show you the right way.

Proverbs 3:5–6 Contemporary English Version (CEV)

5 With all your heart you must trust the LORD AND not your own judgment.
6 Always let him lead you, and he will clear the road for you to follow.

Proverbs 3:5–6 Amplified Bible, Classic Edition (AMPC)

⁵ Lean on, trust in, *and* be confident in the Lord with all your heart *and* mind and do not rely on your own insight *or* understanding.

⁶ In all your ways know, recognize, *and* acknowledge Him, and He will direct *and* make straight *and* plain your paths.

Proverbs 3:5–6 Amplified Bible (AMP)

⁵ Trust in *and* rely confidently on the LORD with all your heart
And do not rely on your own insight *or* understanding.
⁶ [a]In all your ways know *and* acknowledge *and* recognize Him,
And He will make your paths straight *and* smooth [removing obstacles that block your way].

ACKNOWLEDGEMENTS

The stories of this book span over seven decades of my life. I see the people who made them possible as a gift from God, and so my first acknowledgement must be to my God. When I was old enough to realize the part God played in my life, I was awed by the revelation of God's activity in my early youth. His work in my life has allowed me to create profound relationships, and I am forever grateful to those people for their willingness to share their lives and their gifts.

Edward and Hilda Musterer, my parents, not only gave me life; they introduced me to God. Their love and the life lessons they taught me were indispensable in recognizing the value and importance of building a relationship with God. As a child, my mother taught me to pray, and my father instilled within me the joy and value of reading. Their teachings remain with me until this day.

My brother Roy taught me the importance of brotherhood as well as how to maintain a deep, loving relationship through the seasons of life as a family. Even when life's circumstances seemed to be steeped in adversity, he showed me that love and family bonds prevail.

My wife Carol is, as my story attests, a perfect gift from God. She masterfully supports me in my life pursuits, professional engineering and spiritual ministry. I could never have been able to accomplish what I have for fifty years without her love and faithful support.

Randolph Scott "Randy" Musterer, my son, has led me on adventures that have awakened me in ways that no other teacher has done. His focus, patience, and tenacity have been an ongoing inspiration to me as well as to all those that are blessed to be in his life. As God guided me as a father, the path Randy and I walked together has been deep, surprising, and filled with joy.

The countless ministers and church members of the New Apostolic Church have been an ongoing source of guidance and inspiration; I can barely count the blessings held within our encounters.

My many aunts, uncles, and cousins from the two large families of my parents, the Musterers and the Stiers, provided the solid foundation of family love, unity, and faithfulness.

My schoolteachers and college professors, along with my many schoolmates, shaped my joy and hunger for learning and fueled my incessant desire for reading books of diverse subject matter.

The many professional colleagues in the five companies in which I was employed as a professional engineer gave me indispensable opportunities for personal and professional growth that serve me to this day.

My business partner of thirty years, Don A. Bartick, created with me in 1989 an engineering design and development company, 4-Ward Tech, Inc., now 4-Ward Design, Inc. We worked in harmony, bringing intellectual concepts 4-ward to reality, serving the needs of medical and educational institutions, among others.

The wonderful team of volunteers at Garden of Innocence – San Diego and the Garden's founders Elissa Davey and Rebecca

Melendez have opened a whole new ministry for me. Providing dignified burial and funeral services for unidentified and abandoned babies has given me the opportunity to love total strangers and embrace their precious souls.

My writing coach and editor Marni Freedman was indispensable in crafting my detailed chronological stories into a readable manuscript. Marni's ability to teach me how to engage a reader and capture their interest without compromising the essence of a story's message was critical to creating what I feel is a readable, honest, and dynamic presentation of my stories.

Sharon Marta, my cover designer, took Solomon's Recipe's message and created a cover that beams the spirit of God's guidance awaiting to bring a searching soul to the place God needs them to be.

My publisher, Dr. Netreia Carroll and Affordable Publishing, had the much-appreciated patience for me to work through the many months of creating the final manuscript.

Finally, I appreciate the souls whose stories are told in this book. The experiences we shared live within me and will forever. As I recount these experiences, I am moved to profound gratefulness for them and for God who brought us together for a divine outcome.

About the Author

Allan was born in New Jersey in 1943 to loving parents Edward and Hilda. His desire to be an engineer was born when he attended Garfield public schools. Allan received a mechanical engineering degree from Bucknell University in 1965. Employed by Foster Wheeler, a large engineering firm, in nuclear power plant design, he took advanced engineering classes at NJIT before earning an MBA in management from Fairleigh Dickenson University in 1970. Upon graduation, he was sent with his wife Carol to San Diego to support General Atomics nuclear power program. Remaining in San Diego after his assignment, Allan worked for three nuclear-based companies until 1989. Along with a friend and colleague, he founded an engineering company, 4-Ward Design, Inc.

Shortly after arriving in San Diego in 1970, Allan was ordained as a minister in the New Apostolic Church to build a congregation in Claremont and eventually three more congregations. He served occasionally in congregations in the West until he retired in 2008. Before retirement, Allan was led to attend a funeral at Garden of Innocence, an organization providing dignified burials for unidentified and abandoned babies. He is currently Director of Garden of Innocence – San Diego.

In 1973, Allan and Carol welcomed their son Randy into their family. Allan and Randy enjoyed bonding as father and son on a variety of fishing ventures that included deep-sea fishing, trout fishing in a fast stream, and fishing off the coasts of New Jersey, California, and Mexico. Randy, following a thirteen-year career in cancer research, is now the proud owner of two awarded Sushi Restaurants in Silicon Valley.

Allan wrote his first book, *Solomon's Recipe*, with Marni Freedman as his writing coach and mentor. His technical and theological experiences offer a unique melding of his two life perspectives.

The book found its beginnings when Allan was driving to Los Angeles on business and decided to turn off the radio and just think. The result was a retrospective journey into his life from childhood to the present. What he saw was the long string of little moments in his life that were turning points, brief experiences that changed the whole course of his life. Solomon's Recipe was one of those turning points.

CPSIA information can be obtained
at www.ICGtesting.com
Printed in the USA
FSHW011809171019

9 781646 060207